SERIOUS FUN

Other Eye On Education Books
Available from Routledge
www.routledge.com/eyeoneducation

SERIOUS

Practical Strategies to
Motivate and Engage Students

Carolyn Hirst-Loucks
and
Kim P. Loucks

Routledge
Taylor & Francis Group

NEW YORK AND LONDON

First published 2014
by Routledge
711 Third Avenue, New York, NY 10017

and by Routledge
2 Park Square, Milton Park, Abingdon, Oxon OX14 4RN

Routledge is an imprint of the Taylor & Francis Group, an informa business

Library of Congress Cataloging in Publication Data

Hirst-Loucks, Carolyn.
  Serious fun : practical strategies to motivate and engage students
/ by Carolyn Hirst-Loucks and Kim P. Loucks.
  Includes bibliographical references.
    1. Learning. 2. Motivation in education. 3. Activity programs in
education. I. Title.
  LB1060.H57 2013
  370.15'4--dc23   2013014021

ISBN: 978-1-59667-253-6 (pbk)
ISBN: 978-1-315-85228-7 (ebk)

Typeset in Palatino by Rick Soldin

Disclaimer and Request for Information

Every effort has been made to properly cite and credit those who created the activities and strategies in this book. The authors apologize for any oversight in giving proper credit. Please contact the authors and the publisher so that they might be corrected in the future.

Printed and bound in the United States of America by Publishers Graphics,
LLC on sustainably sourced paper.

"In every conceivable manner,
the family is link to our past,
bridge to our future."

Alex Haley

This book is dedicated to our parents, E. John Loucks, and in loving memory, John and Ruth Hirst and Patricia Loucks. They encouraged us to be readers and leaders, life-long learners and to always follow our passions. Our parents loved, supported, and expected us to be good people who play nicely and work hard. They unwaveringly believed we could do anything if we only worked at it—a life lesson that fortunately stuck.

Contents

8 Seriously Fun Strategies for Movement 83

9 Seriously Fun Strategies for Closure 91

10 Seriously Fun Content-Specific Activities 101

About the Authors

Carolyn Hirst-Loucks and Mr. Kim Loucks have had extensive experience in a variety of educational settings. The bulk of their classroom experience is teaching at the middle level. They love that age group ... seriously! Carolyn and Kim were administrators, working in district-level roles as well as providing staff development. Currently they represent *Teaching and Learning Connected (TLC)*, an educational consulting firm focused on providing high-quality professional development on a variety of exciting and innovative topics. The Louckses are also the authors of *Study Strategies for Student Success*©.

Ms. Hirst-Loucks and Mr. Loucks are graduates of colleges within the State University of New York system, Carolyn with a Bachelor of Science degree in Education, Kim a Bachelor of Arts in Mathematics. They each have a Master of Science degree in Education as well as a Certificate of Advanced Study in Educational Administration.

Carolyn and Kim truly believe that the ultimate keys to success lie not so much in covering curriculum as in engaging young people in their learning. Through the use of seriously fun strategies students will acquire content and skills that allow them to uncover a wealth of knowledge and learning, leading to unprecedented levels of success.

Carolyn and Kim can be contacted through their website, www.tlconnected.com and by email at teachingandlearningconnected@gmail.com

Acknowledgments

Ralph Waldo Emerson said, "Cultivate the habit of being grateful for every good thing that comes to you, and give thanks continuously." Many people have been instrumental in bringing this book to life and we are grateful for their help and continually give thanks.

We express our unending gratitude to all those with whom we had the honor and privilege to work throughout our careers. We thank all the students, staff members, colleagues, mentors, and friends from the Union Springs and Weedsport Central School Districts as well as our colleagues and associates from the Auburn Enlarged City School District, Cayuga-Onondaga Board of Cooperative Educational Services (BOCES), and Onondaga-Cortland-Madison BOCES. We are also appreciative of the thoughts and ideas gained from participants in our professional development sessions. We learn every day from *you* through our interactions.

Thanks to all those people that encouraged and provided assistance and guidance through their support, and all of our friends and colleagues who read, offered comments, edited, and proofread. We give special credit to Leela George, Denise Hudson, Ann Mahanna, and Tiffany Squires, who provided a second set of eyes and a sounding board for our ideas.

Recognition must go to Lauren Beebe, who constantly provided encouragement, advice, and expertise. She helped to smooth the road before us. We offer our heartfelt appreciation to, Robert Sickles at Eye On Education, for offering us the chance to share with others our passion about students, fun, and learning.

Seriously, this has been a fun project that we couldn't have done alone. Our gratitude knows no bounds. Thank you all.

Chapter 1

What Is Serious Fun in the Classroom All About?

Above all, life, and school, should be fun ... seriously.
—Anonymous

"Above all, life, and school, *should* be fun." That quote *has* to kindle your curiosity. School? Fun? Yes! If we can pretty much agree that life should be fun, then why not school? And we believe it's important to be very serious about that fun.

Life *is* fun, and we see that so readily in our young people ... mostly outside of school. Picture this scenario: it's the third day of a week-long vacation at the beach. A large, extended family, which includes lots of young people, has come together for a reunion. A collective cry rises up, and, in unison, "WE'RE BORED!" echoes among the children. They whine to their parents about going back to the cottage to play video games. That doesn't work. The curt, adult reply is "Just go play in the sand."

Left to their own devices, the children gather together and hatch a scheme to create the most elaborate sand castle on the beach. They swing into action and began working together using shovels, buckets, and scoops. Natural leaders emerge from within the group, take over, and prompt the other workers. "Put more sand right there." "This is sooo much fun." "Dig the channel deeper in the outside moat." "That's perfect, Kevin." The sounds of hard work punctuated with frequent laughter and squeals of delight begin to overpower the sound of the wind and surf.

Throughout the afternoon, every child plays a role in the construction of the grand castle, including its complex system of moats. Building and rebuilding are a constant theme as the children make changes and adjustments. As beach-goers watch the children hard at work all afternoon, they can see the children's faces scrunched in determination, hear the urgency in their voices as they shout directions to one another, and feel the excitement generated by the children's play and hard work. When the tide rushes in, the moats fill and the castle stands, amid the cheers of the adults and the children. Through play, a group of children move from bored, disengaged, and uninterested to energized, enthralled, and excited. And they do it on their own!

Examining how this scenario might translate into the classroom setting is worthy of our attention. There are times when students are reluctant learners—unmotivated and nonparticipatory. School is a serious place where people work hard in order to learn. However, serious work does not have to mean dreary and dour. Educators who understand the role that serious fun can have in learning work very hard to provide their students opportunities to be meaningfully involved in the learning process. This collaborative learning environment is punctuated with problem solving, exploration, creativity, and, ultimately, a higher likelihood of success.

The probability and degree of student learning increases when students work as collaborative problem solvers and are considered equal learning partners with their teacher. Students are motivated to learn when lessons are intentionally designed with seriously fun strategies and activities. When instructors create lessons that are engaging and focused on critical content and skills, students retain new knowledge at a higher rate because the lessons are meaningful and motivating. It is for this reason educators should consider filling the learning environment with serious fun.

What Is Serious Fun in the Classroom?

It's a learning environment where academics are rigorous, students are engaged, and learning is clearly evident. The classroom setting is such that the activities and strategies employed promote higher-level thinking to gain knowledge. There is excitement, conversation, movement, and, from time to time, laughter permeating the room. A seriously fun classroom is *not* always "laugh out loud" funny. It *is* dynamic and a place where students are engaged, relaxed, and free to laugh. When the element of fun is infused into learning and the surroundings are rich with hard work and enthusiasm, students are more likely to learn and remember what they learn.

For some, a list of criteria is helpful in defining and understanding a concept. While not a checklist, the bulleted items below may be helpful in describing a seriously fun classroom. Serious fun looks different from one classroom to another and can change from day to day. There is no one-size-fits-all or cookie-cutter approach. Seriously fun teachers will vary in their lesson designs and in their approach to reaching their objectives. Some of the items on this list may be present in an individual teacher's classroom and some will not. The degree to which some criteria exist will vary as well. For example, in a seriously fun classroom, depending on the teacher's objectives, a visitor might see everyone moving about the room at the same time, students working with a single partner, or small groups of students excitedly playing an academically rich, content-related game. This list is meant merely as a guide to assist in planning.

A seriously fun classroom

- clearly connects to content
- engages students
- motivates learners
- fosters collaboration
- uses open-ended questions, prompts, and/or problems
- offers choice
- encourages movement
- provides opportunities for reflection
- promotes higher-level thinking (analysis, synthesis, evaluation)
- includes real-world and relevant activities
- cultivates laughter, humor, play ... and fun!

Let there be no doubt. The work of learning in our schools is serious stuff. Given the reality of local, state, and national mandates, the focus on 21st-century skills, the Common Core State Standards Initiative, standardized assessments, and implications for teacher evaluation, it's critical that teachers strive to provide a high-quality, standards-based learning environment for their class. They need to be continually on the lookout for strategies and ideas that will help them to help their learners be more successful.

The strategies included in *Serious Fun* promote academic rigor while attending to the social and emotional needs of the young people in our charge. A number of these strategies can also be used to facilitate learning and conversation with adults at team, faculty, and leadership meetings. Each strategy is explained in narrative form. The discussion of some strategies will offer a brief example from a particular content area, and others suggest how to use that strategy as formative assessment.

Appendix A will be a valuable resource since it lists the strategies in alphabetical order in chart form. A brief summary is offered, along with codes pertaining to cost, preparation time, classroom time and the page number on which the complete strategy can be found. You might want to bookmark this chart.

One of the primary responsibilities of every educator is to learn how, when, where, and why to adapt or adopt a particular idea or strategy. Finding something that fits perfectly and can be readily adopted can be a real challenge. Perhaps that will happen with a few of the ideas put forth in *Serious Fun*. More likely, it's adaptation that will rule the day. For example, in Chapter 8, you'll read how a particular strategy, *Baggage Claim*, might be used in a third-grade, English language arts classroom. However, if you teach middle school science, you can take the basic tenets of the strategy and make the necessary adaptations so that they can be used effectively for your specific grade level and content area. When you make those important modifications, you'll find that *Baggage Claim* still "works" just fine. In fact, it might be even more effective since it has been tailored for your specific class, thus maximizing the learning and ultimately increasing the likelihood of success. This will hold true for nearly all the strategies shared in this book.

Let's take a peek into one school and three different classrooms:

> Mr. Serious is just that. His students come to class on time. They are well-behaved and orderly, compliant. They appear to be attentive. The students sit in neat rows, taking notes as Mr. Serious lectures for thirty-five minutes. Homework is assigned. The next day, this pattern is repeated and pretty much continues that way for much of the school year. Tests are viewed as a critical part of class and taken

seriously. Most students score well on tests, mostly relying on short-term memory to respond to literal-level questions. When interviewed about Mr. Serious's classroom, students say "Boring," "I could have just read my textbook," and "We never have any fun." By the end of the semester, they generally remember very little about the content and, sadly, may have *learned* very little.

Down the hall is the classroom of Ms. Fun, with a capital F! She believes in the power that fun can have in helping students learn. While she is an advocate of discovery learning, there is little evidence that it exists in her classroom. Ms. Fun's classroom is disorganized, chaotic, and quite loud. Activities on a variety of topics are laid out around the room. Students move freely from one spot to another, constantly chatting with friends, although seldom about the learning objectives for the day. When interviewed about Ms. Fun's classroom, students say, "It's a break from so many of my other classes," "I get to talk to all my friends," and "I am nervous about the big tests at the end of the year because we never seem to focus on important stuff." They remember the games they played very clearly, yet can demonstrate only some of the learning from them.

Across the hall is the classroom of Mr. Serious Fun. Early in his career, Mr. SF often struggled because of his unfamiliarity with what a seriously fun classroom might look like. He wanted to implement strategies and activities he was sure would lead to greater success for his students and for him, but he couldn't find the right balance. By reflecting on his practice, connecting with mentors, and persevering, he discovered *some* of the secrets to success. He continues to learn and grow, and now his room is alive with learning. Students are working in small groups on a teacher-generated task that completely captures their interest. Small groups of students are gathered in different locations in the classroom. They cluster around large sheets of paper that contain different categories/topics related to the content they are currently studying. As the principal steps into the classroom, she talks with students and asks them what they are doing. She can clearly see students engaged in conversations around the topics on the posters.

From time to time, Mr. Serious Fun stops and shares with his students important information about what's coming next. It is evident that his students are having fun *and* are able to discuss exactly what they are learning and/or why they are learning it. When interviewed about Mr. Serious Fun's classroom, they say, "We can really tell Mr. SF is serious about our learning," "It was great to work and play with my friends," and "I actually know this stuff!" Thanks to his hard work, reflection, and success, he finds himself mentoring colleagues as they embark on their journeys of creating their own seriously fun classrooms.

As you reflect on these three teachers (and those with whom you work or have worked), you'll see very different styles and approaches. All these teachers believe they are doing what's best for students. Mr. Serious views himself as the expert in the room, the only person who possesses knowledge and answers. He is certain that it is his sole responsibility to give that knowledge to his students. Ms. Fun acts as a bystander, simply watching her students "play." Her laissez-faire approach centers around the belief that if she provides fun activities for her students, they will learn. Both these teachers operate under the assumption, "If I teach it, they'll learn it."

However, it's Mr. Serious Fun who has engaged his learners as he employs strategies that allow them to succeed. He designs activities that capitalize on what we know constitutes good learning. He facilitates the flow of the lesson in an environment conducive to learning. Mr. SF monitors and adjusts throughout the class period. He, too, is engaged and having fun along with his students. He models for his students how a good learner behaves by constantly asking himself, "How can I make this even better?"

Why Infuse Fun into Something as Serious as School?

This is an essential question that should be considered by educators everywhere. Teachers like Mr. Serious Fun use this question as a springboard for being reflective practitioners. They design lessons that include strategies to infuse fun into the learning process, engaging students and motivating them to participate in the acquisition of content and skills necessary to be productive citizens in the 21st century.

So are schools selling the right bill of goods to their customers? A growing number of these customers were born in the 21st century, while those who teach them are from the 20th century. Our students make the conscious choice every day to buy (or not to buy) the products we are trying to sell them. A good part of the research about serious fun in the classroom comes from the 20th century (or earlier). However, the skills found in a seriously fun classroom support students who will work and play in the 21st century. Their success depends on these skills:

- thinking critically and making judgments
- solving complex, multidisciplinary, open-ended problems
- being creative and thinking entrepreneurially
- communicating and collaborating
- making innovative use of knowledge, information and opportunities
- taking charge of financial, health and civic responsibilities. (Partnership for 21st Century Skills, 2008)

If we truly believe that serious fun promotes creativity, problem solving, application of knowledge to real life, collaboration, and good communication, then these 21st-century skills provide the justification needed to convince those who question the role fun has in learning. Throughout this entire book, the reader will find that 21st-century skills are addressed and supported through the use of the strategies and ideas suggested.

A sizable body of research demonstrates the power, impact, and importance of play and fun in learning. While research will be noted in this book, the primary focus of *Serious Fun* will be descriptions and illustrations of strategies that actively engage students while infusing academically rich fun into the learning environment. Using information from this book, a teacher will be able to design lessons incorporating strategies and activities that promote students' use of higher-level thinking to gain important content knowledge. It isn't necessary to be a comedian. Success comes from looking at content and skills and finding ways to get students more engaged with their learning.

The Common Core State Standards Initiative (CCSSI) integrates 21st-century skills throughout its K–12 approach to teaching and learning. For example, the CCSSI portrait of students who meet standards are those who demonstrate independence, have strong content knowledge, respond to varying demands, and understand other perspectives (CCSSI, 2010). These are all attributes of learners engaged in classroom activities that are seriously fun. These attributes are fostered through the teacher's intentional use of fun instructional strategies and activities when designing lessons.

Included in the language of the Standards for Mathematical Practice (SMP) from the Common Core State Standards (CCSS) are phrases such as "make sense of problems and persevere in solving them," "reason abstractly," "construct viable arguments," and "attend to precision" (CCSSI, 2010). The SMPs are integrated throughout the content standards for mathematics. When students are "playing" with content in the classroom, they are doing all this … and more.

With the continued focus on high-stakes tests, students and teachers become weary of a drill-and-kill environment where too often rote memory responses to literal-level questions seem to be the safe route to success. Examine the two scenarios from a mathematics classroom below. If you were a student in *your* classroom, which would you prefer?

- Students are given a worksheet with twenty problems asking them to calculate the volume of different three-dimensional figures.
- Students are given a real-life problem their teacher faces. Due to recent renovations in her kitchen, she lost about 20 percent of the space she previously had in her pantry. This loss is forcing her to be more mindful and economical about her storage space. Her question to students is simple and straightforward: "Which type of container, cylindrical, like a soup can, or rectangular prisms, like a box of cookies, should I use to best accommodate my new, smaller space?"

The first choice will produce twenty correct answers, most of them obtained by simply applying a formula to calculate volume. In the second choice, the content is exactly the same: volume. There are multiple correct and viable solutions, yet the nature of the problem is likely to be more engaging and, perhaps, more fun for students. In addition, students get the chance to connect with their teacher while solving a real-life situation, thereby establishing relationships between teacher and students. While the problem in the second choice isn't laugh-out-loud funny, it is an example of serious fun, especially compared to the alternative.

Unfortunately, it has been found that if students spend too much time doing work like the twenty problems on the worksheet, they often struggle to apply their knowledge to new, unique, real-life situations. Far too often, school becomes drudgery and students check out, emotionally and/or physically. Some choose to remain in school, although they have dropped out emotionally. They go through the motions; they "do" school, yet see little or no value in what they are supposed to be doing. They are disengaged and marking time until they can move on to the next level—life beyond their public school experience. However, if teachers employ seriously fun strategies to teach key concepts and skills, learning becomes fun, students can transfer their knowledge and make thoughtful responses to new situations, and, in the end, they are motivated to stay in school.

It's the excitement, energy, enthusiasm, and hard work we saw in the children at the beach in our opening story that educators would love to see in their classrooms. The point of the story is not for teachers to dump truckloads of sand in the classroom and have the students go at it. Professionals must consider the learning that is essential for grade-level content and then explore how to best integrate serious fun into curriculum, instruction, and assessment. These seriously fun activities and strategies hook all learners so that they are open to the joy and passion of learning.

Teaching is a complicated endeavor involving a multitude of elements. Teaching in a seriously fun classroom is no more or less complicated. *Serious Fun* offers research to support the use of fun, humor, and play in learning, detailing how this approach supports the Common Core State Standards and 21st-century skills. However, the bulk of this book is dedicated to strategies that promote and support a seriously fun learning environment. *All* the strategies put forth in *Serious Fun* have the flexibility and adaptability to be successfully implemented at almost *any* point in a lesson, in almost *any* content, and at almost *any* grade level. As a professional, you can adapt the strategies, and the steps needed to integrate them within the lesson, to fit your own students' needs. *Serious Fun* offers the reader some of the essential pieces necessary to design quality instruction. This book is not composed of step-by-step, minute-to-minute, detailed lesson plans.

Teachers might consider these specific strategies when designing their lessons and administrators could use them when working with their staff. The reader will find many content-specific suggestions and, in Appendix D, a few detailed lesson plans. The intent of *Serious Fun* is to provide educators with ideas that will enhance and fit nicely with the work already being done.

So what's serious fun in the classroom all about? To help you begin to think about your answer to this question, consider these tips:

> **S**elect fun activities that have essential content and skills as the primary focus.
>
> **E**xpect a little chaos. When children play and have fun, things can get a little messy.
>
> **R**igor and high standards should be the number-one priority of instruction.
>
> **I**nvite change. Within change, there is challenge.
>
> **O**vert observation of student engagement and interest is crucial.
>
> **U**nexpected learnings will occur … and this is generally a good thing.
>
> **S**ystemically use humor and fun in all content areas.
>
> **F**ind opportunities for students to work collaboratively and have fun together.
>
> **U**se what you already have. Celebrate and capitalize on what you are doing *now*.
>
> **N**ext steps? Where will you go next and how will you get there?

As you begin the process of infusing serious fun into your learning environment, think about what you already do. Build on your strengths. You'll soon find that serious fun in the classroom is all about what you do and what you know, enhanced by what you'll learn from the information in this book. Identify the strategies, ideas, suggestions, and tips that look interesting, would work for you and your students, or seem like they just might be fun. Take those ever-important baby steps as you blend the new with the known. Self-assess. Keep plenty of reflective notes so that you can tweak and tailor the strategies to best fit you and your students. Consider how you can infuse serious fun into each lesson and before you know it you will be getting the ha-ha's leading to the aha's.

Seriously, folks, this should be a lot of fun …

Chapter 2

What Does the Research Say About Serious Fun?

Play is the highest form of research.
—Albert Einstein

ou're set and ready to go. You've established a goal for the upcoming school year to lay the foundation for a seriously fun atmosphere in your classroom. Throughout the summer you prepared for success by systematically reviewing and tweaking your lesson plans. You verified that your objectives are clearly established and then purposefully redesigned your lessons to include activities that are more motivating and fun. The school year begins and you are feeling success. "This is going to be great!" you say to yourself (and perhaps out loud to others). As you reflect and compare this class to previous ones, the students seem to be more collaborative, there is less stress, and your students' conversation and examination of the concepts and skills are at a much higher level then you have ever experienced.

The school year is progressing nicely. Late October arrives and you prepare for parent conferences. Sitting in front of you is a parent whose opening statement is, "I'm not sure what you are doing. Joshua says that he has fun every day in your classroom. Fun is fine, but he's not going to be tested on fun. I'm concerned that he is not learning what he needs so that he can do well on tests." How do you respond?

A week or so after parent conferences, you stop outside the faculty room to chat with a student. The conversation ended, with your hand on the doorknob, you overhear Mr. Serious loudly proclaiming to colleagues, "I don't know what is going on in that classroom. Certainly no learning. Students are up and about; she is not at the front of the room teaching. I just know her students' scores are going to be miserable, bringing down the pass rate of the entire department. I can't wait until she is observed." How do you respond?

Shortly thereafter, the principal sticks her head in the doorway of your classroom and asks if she can speak to you at the end of the day. You go to the meeting expecting to discuss your renewed love for teaching, your higher expectations for learning, and the positive feedback from students. Instead, her question is, "Do you need more help and support this year? I notice that as I walk by there is much more noise and movement in your room than in the past. If you've got some behavior problems, maybe we can work together to get you back on the right track." How do you respond?

The fear of many parents and educators is the perception that if students in the classroom are having fun, then learning isn't really taking place. Because of a lack of knowledge, outsiders (and some insiders) in education believe that when students are engaged in activities that are fun they cannot be engaged with rigorous content and skills. These beliefs can manifest themselves in questions such as "Won't children be best served if teachers do their job by providing the students with information and they just learn it?" "Don't students learn best in a setting where lecture and worksheets that specifically target what will be on the end-of-the-year assessment reign?" Let's explore some of the research that will allow these questions to be answered.

The Seriously Fun Human Brain

To begin to answer these questions, we'll examine some of the latest brain research. Dr. Judy Willis, a noted neurologist, teacher, and author, explains that in a classroom setting, when the human brain takes in information, it first goes to a group of nuclei in the center of the brain called the amygdala (Willis, 2011). The amygdala is connected to the prefrontal cortex, an area involved with our highest intellectual properties. Acting as a clearinghouse for incoming information, the amygdala's primary role is to sort and select where memories associated with events are stored. Sensory inputs are constantly being sent and received. When the amygdala receives them, it decides in which part of the brain the new information is to reside (Gogolla et al., 2009).

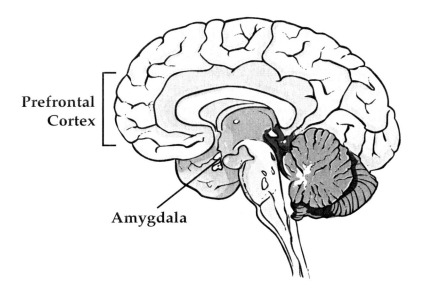

Prefrontal Cortex

Amygdala

The amygdala is a part of the limbic system, making it a component of an active vigilance-for-survival mechanism. This part of the brain processes and retains new learning much more efficiently when it is not under stress. Dr. Willis, unfortunately, found that when a student is bored and disengaged, the brain acts as though it is under stress. The amygdala becomes more hyperactive and is unable to process the information effectively. That part of the brain defaults back to the animal brain, which determines whether the body should be in flight, fight, or freeze mode. When this happens, new information is not sent to a part of the brain where it can be readily stored and retrieved for further use. Think back to Mr. Serious's classroom. The students' reactions to Mr. Serious's instruction were due to the fact that they were bored and couldn't remember the material taught. Those students' brains were treating the situation as stressful. In this state, the brain shuts down the thinking process, freezing, and reverts to flight or fight. While students aren't likely to immediately bolt from the room (we hope), they might ask for permission to go to the bathroom or their locker. Some brains will react to the stress auditorily: "I've had enough of this!" In situations such as this, a disciplinary issue escalates. Current brain research would support the responses of these students.

So how do we break this cycle and ensure students are not bored? We most definitely, and perhaps most importantly, want to know that students are actually learning. Because our most reluctant learners are bored and disengaged, their amygdalae are in a constant state of stress. To counteract this stress, the instructor must consider the concepts and skills to be taught and purposefully design lessons that are novel and/or have an element of fun. William Danforth, founder of Nestlé Purina, said, "The best cure for a sluggish mind is to disturb its routine." To translate this into classroom practice, instructional strategies need to be varied. The brain loves to mix things up. Novelty and variety lead to a more engaged student. If the student is actively engaged, the amygdala is relaxed and can route incoming information to places where it can be stored and then retrieved later (Willis, 2012). The brain functions better and is able to make connections between the new learning and the known, cementing the information more solidly in long-term memory.

In a 2004 *Education Week* article, "Feel-Bad Education," Alfie Kohn posits that "richer thinking is more likely to occur in an atmosphere of *exuberant discovery,* the kind of place where kids plunge into their projects and can't wait to pick up where they left off yesterday" (Kohn, 2004; emphasis added). It would certainly be incredible if the norm for classrooms was an atmosphere of exuberant discovery.

If It's Good Enough for Them ...

Many successful businesses credit fun as a reason for some of their achievements. Often we hear and read in the popular media that things would be better in schools if educators followed a business model. In some cases, like the businesses mentioned in the following paragraphs, we are inclined to agree.

If a random group of people were asked, "Do you believe that Google is a successful business?" just about everyone would respond in the affirmative. In 2012, *Fortune Magazine* named Google the #1 best company for which to work. Another company, Universum, surveyed nearly 60,000 undergraduate students and asked them to name their "ideal" employers upon graduation; Google claimed the top spot (Levering & Moskowitz, 2012). Google employs about 30,000 people worldwide and in 2011 created more than 7,000 new positions, for which it had more than a million applicants (Casserly, 2012). Clearly Google is offering what people want. One of the reasons for this tremendous applicant-to-job ratio is the work environment. Google contracts with designers to create campuses and offices infused with fun and support for its workers. For example, the lobby of a Google building in Australia looks like a rain forest with a rusted Google logo peeking out. In London, the work area resembles a resort area known as Brighton Beach. Google management believes that if the employees are in a fun environment they will be more creative, more collaborative, and more likely to persevere in solving problems or designing new products. When the workers' normal routine is disrupted, minds are opened. Looking at the bottom line, fun makes a difference to Google ... and the millions upon millions of those who utilize its services.

Imagine if this was *your* classroom. Someone walking in would see that it is bright, colorful, and connected in some way to the students who "work" there. Interesting displays, student work, cartoons, and photos all connect the student to the learning environment. Adults enthusiastically greet students at the door with a warm smile and a cheery hello. Relationships build between the teacher and the students. When there is a strong personal connection, the student is more inclined to focus and be ready to do the hard work and deep thinking that are required of collaborative problem solvers.

In 2009 Volkswagen created the "Fun Theory" (Fun Theory, 2012), based on a core belief that people will do the right thing—use the stairs rather than the escalator, drive at the speed limit, recycle, pick up trash, buckle their seatbelts—if there is an element of fun involved. Each year, Fun Theory sponsors a contest in which people are invited to submit their ideas for new promotions. One is ultimately selected as the best of the field. The fun is often simple. The very first Fun Theory project was the installation of the Piano Stairs in Stockholm in 2009. A broad set of stairs parallel to an escalator was converted into a working piano. When a person used the stairs, each step played a musical note when stepped on. The video of the Stockholm Piano Stairs captured people's attention and went viral. The video hit 3.3 million views on YouTube in less than two weeks and went on to collect more blog posts and Twitter-mentions than any other viral video ever posted. And it worked: over the next few days, 66 percent more people took the stairs over the adjacent escalator.

What might the Fun Theory look like in a classroom? Homework can be the standard "Read pages 156 to 170 and answer in complete sentences Questions 1 to 5 at the end of the reading." Or it could be "Reflect upon our learning today and, using your text as a resource, create two truths and one fib about the causes of World War II. Tomorrow at the beginning of class we'll share with one another." Which homework assignment do you think will have the higher compliance rate? (For other suggestions, see "How to Break Out of the Homework Rut!" in Appendix B.) Remember, according to the Fun Theory, you should make something fun if you want people to do it.

If you have ever traveled on Southwest Airlines, you have seen evidence of serious fun at work. Typically, your experience is pleasurable and you enjoy your trip. At the very beginning of the trip, as early in the process as check-in, you're greeted by employees dressed in wacky costumes and balloons waving above the counter, setting the mood for your trip. Once you're seated on the plane, the flight attendants go through the crucial safety information sometimes in song or maybe even in rap, but definitely not the way you're used to: droning on about important rules and regulations while some passengers pay little heed, many don't hear, and still others simply zone out, missing the message entirely. These innovations at Southwest are based on the company's foundational belief: "We at Southwest Airlines foster and embrace fun, creativity, individuality, and empowerment. We love our employees. We trust our employees" (West, 2005).

It's important to note that Southwest Airlines has consistently been one of the most profitable airlines, in part because of its core beliefs. In 2012 the airline was named by Forbes one of the top ten best travel companies to work for (Smith, 2012). It also has one of the highest employee satisfaction ratings. Many people have come to believe that to be professional one cannot have humor and fun in the workplace, as it might be viewed as unprofessional and inappropriate. Southwest Airlines is an example of a company that has distanced itself from that attitude. Its management believes that a lack of humor in the workplace drains its employees and causes them to be dissatisfied. Encouraging employees to have fun at work and to use humor in their dealings with one another and with their customers allows the company to grow. Southwest Airlines has seen productivity, creativity, adaptability, morale, and the bottom line all increase, even during times of economic strain. Because the employees are happy in their positions, the retention rate is very high (Freiberg & Freiberg, 1998). Colleen Barrett, President Emerita of Southwest Airlines, coauthored with Ken Blanchard *Lead with LUV* (Blanchard and Barrett, 2010) in which she outlines her business philosophy: "Lead with love, appreciate people, they'll come alive and you'll get great results."

Let's see what you might do if you assumed the role of a Southwest employee in your classroom: On the first day of school, you stand at the door, greeting students and inviting them to be a part of the classroom, treating them like welcome guests. To reinforce the culture of a warm, accepting classroom where attention to studies is important, an English language arts teacher might begin the school year with a lesson that is seriously fun—for example, reading to the students from Dr. Seuss's book *Oh, the Places You'll Go!* When Seuss's main character says, "life may be a 'Great Balancing Act,' but through it all 'There's fun to be done,'" the opportunity opens for a conversation among students about what this phrase might mean for the upcoming year. What parallels can be made between the students and the journey upon which they are about to embark? This activity sets a tone that is much different from the routine of assigning seats, explaining classroom rules, and issuing textbooks. Students take part in conversations with one another that, with the right questions, allow them to engage in higher-level thinking right from the start.

This same approach works very well in a mathematics classroom. For efficiency and in order to get to know students by name, teachers typically call the students' names off a roster and place each student in an assigned seat. In a seriously fun middle school mathematics classroom, you might label the desks with coordinate axes. You give the entering students a slip with their name on it and a pair of coordinates and ask them to find their assigned seats. The process actively engages students with content by encouraging collaboration and communication and sets the tone for the year. It is a great way to start the school year—the unspoken message sent to students is that we will work on content and it will be seriously fun.

Southwest Airlines believes that the safety message before takeoff is important, so maybe, just maybe, if they package it in a fun way, the passengers will pay attention and remember key points in case of an emergency. Our classrooms can start to work like this if we present important content and skills in a way that is fun and engaging enough to get our "customers" to pay attention. Theodor Seuss Geisel, a.k.a. Dr. Seuss, once said, "A person's a person, no matter how small. Children want the same things we want. To laugh, to be challenged, to be entertained and delighted." Serious fun!

Consider the questions asked in the beginning of this chapter. "Won't children be best served if teachers do their job by providing the students with information and they just learn it?" "Don't students learn best in a setting where lecture and worksheets that specifically target what will be on the end-of-the-year assessment reign?"

C.W. Metcalf, a noted humorist who works primarily in the business field, calls this type of thinking "terminal professionalism" (Metcalf and Felible, 1992). To illustrate the phrase, visualize what you would see if you were a fly on a wall of a large office. The atmosphere is very serious, stern, and stoic. The terminal professionals, employees, are definitely not having fun. Some appear to be visibly stressed, taking on more work and working many more hours than in the past. You can surely conjure up images of this happening in our schools. Perhaps you even know a few terminal professionals.

An example of terminal professionalism is the advice given to many new teachers: "Don't smile until Christmas." Do you know people who believe that fun, humor, and play in a classroom setting are unprofessional and unproductive? Ken Blanchard, in a video promoting *Lead with LUV* (Blanchard and Barrett, 2011), remarks that we often treat those who are closest to us worse than new acquaintances. You may remember from past experiences a classroom teacher who, because of the way she treated you or talked to you, did not seem to value you as a student ... or as a person. Just think of the impact this might have on the learning process.

The Mental and Physical Health Benefits of a Serious Fun Classroom

You've got to be there to learn. If students are not in school, then the chances that they will be able to learn essential concepts and skills are lessened. This just makes sense, right? Let's explore the health benefits of laughter and fun in a classroom, for both student and teacher.

Think back to the last time you watched *Mary Poppins*. Remember when Mary and Bert visit Uncle Albert and sing "I Love to Laugh"?

> We love to laugh
> Loud and long and clear
> We love to laugh
> So ev'rybody can hear
> The more you laugh
> The more you fill with glee
> And the more the glee
> The more we're a merrier we!

> (*Mary Poppins: An Original Walt Disney Recordings Soundtrack*)

Mary, Bert, and Uncle Albert were certainly not stressed. Many of our students and teachers are under a lot of stress. There is an increased emphasis placed on students to perform well on the unending stream of tests being administered in our schools. This pressure on students, at all levels, pressure that previously was not as pronounced, permeates 21st-century classrooms. At the secondary level, students are under pressure to perform so that they can get into the right college following graduation. Laughter might be just what the doctor ordered.

Laughter is a stress reliever. When a person laughs, the level of stress hormones like cortisol, epinephrine (adrenaline), dopamine, and growth hormone is reduced. Some stress is good, but if you are constantly on edge because of excessive stress, it can lead to serious health problems, such as heart disease, sleep problems, digestive trouble, depression, obesity, and memory impairment. That's because your body's fight-flight-or-freeze reaction is constant. Your body acts as though there is a continuous threat to its well-being. When you laugh, stress hormones decrease, the level of health-enhancing hormones like endorphins and neurotransmitters increases, and you are able to block pain and increase pleasure (Smith & Segal, 2012). Perfect for the classroom!

Laughter gives you a stronger immune system, as well as fewer physical effects of stress. Laughter increases the number of antibody-producing cells and enhances the effectiveness of T cells. T cells are lymphocytes, special cells that destroy other cells that have been infected or somehow changed in the body. T cells remove antigens that have been tagged by antibodies as a foreign substance in the body. That's why some T cells are actually called "killer cells."

Dr. Steven Sultanoff, former president of the American Association for Applied and Therapeutic Humor, says that laughter is like internal jogging. As you laugh, you take in more oxygen than you can use; it is almost as though you are hyperventilating for a very short time. This extra oxygen goes directly to your cells and major organs, like the lungs, heart, and brain. Who can argue with getting more oxygen to the brain? In some big cities there are actually businesses that cater to this idea. For the going rate of about a dollar a minute, you can purchase highly pure oxygen (about 92 percent) at an oxygen bar. After a typical fifteen-minute session, patrons say they feel an increased sense of relaxation, reduced stress, heightened mental clarity, and a feeling of being ready for anything that life will serve up.

In addition to an increase in oxygen intake, your body temperature, metabolism, heart rate, and pulse also increase. And you don't even have to lace up your sneakers.

In 2004, Maciej Buchowski, Director of Bionutrition at Vanderbilt University Medical Center, and senior research specialist Karen Majchrzak completed a study that found that laughing increases a person's heart rate 10 to 20 percent (Colmenares, 2005). Extrapolating the data, Buchowski and Majchrzak found that ten to fifteen minutes of laughter a day could increase an average person's energy expenditure by ten to forty calories, which translates into about four pounds a year. We're all familiar with the phrase, "I laughed so hard it hurt." Think about all the muscles used when you laugh. It's a workout. Your body shakes, the muscles in your face are in motion, your abdomen tightens, your shoulders move up and down. No gym fees, no instructors, no scheduling times. You carry the means with you everywhere—just laugh!

As we've just explored, a lot of activity goes on in the body during laughter. Once you stop laughing, the physiological benefits continue. Think about how you feel after a hearty laugh. You might be physically wiped out; you might even be limp because of all of the muscles involved. After laughing, the body goes into a more relaxed state that can last up to forty-five minutes. During this time, the heart rate, respiratory rate, and blood pressure decrease to lower levels. Your body zoomed from zero to sixty in record time and then was cut off. This cooling-down period relieves stress and clears your mind, readying you for whatever's coming next.

In addition to the physical benefits, laughter in the classroom has social and emotional benefits as well. Laughter is contagious; the group becomes more cohesive. Laughter is universal; there is no need to translate. There is a shared bond among students that opens the pathway to better communication and collaboration, cornerstones in the problem-solving process. This bond acts as a strong buffer against what might happen in the future. It goes a very long way in forging the strong relationships crucial for success in today's classrooms. The stress level is lowered and the neural pathways in students' brains open up, resulting in better thinking. Students are more eager to be physically present and ready to learn in a classroom where humor and laughter are encouraged.

Selma Wassermann, Professor Emeritus at Simon Fraser University in British Columbia, Canada, believes that "with play teachers can have it all. [They] should free themselves from the safe and secure road, and open classrooms to the more messy, the more generative, the more original, the more delightful world of play as a means of learning about the world" (Wassermann, 1992). Students are more likely to be autonomous, confident, empowered learners in a seriously fun classroom. They are open and ready to explore the possibilities of content. Creativity comes from messing around, tinkering with what is known, doing something new. This in turn opens doors to an even deeper exploration of content. Teachers in seriously fun classrooms who go about their day with their door wide open offer students and adults a peek into a classroom that entices students to join in the fun, in the learning. The seriously fun teacher creates a reason for students to want to be in that classroom.

Music to Our Ears (and Minds)

If laughter is truly the best medicine, then another prescription that enhances the classroom learning climate is the use of music. Plato recognized that music "is a more potent instrument than any other for education" (Harris, 2009, p. xi). Music is found in every culture and is one of the first means used to help a child learn. Think back for a moment how you learned the alphabet (you are probably singing it right now!). Is it even possible to recite the alphabet without singing, even if it's to yourself? Many of the rhymes we learned as children were learned through the use of song. Lullabies are part of childhood. The power that music has for developing literacy is almost unparalleled. The use of music helps children to learn through experimentation with rhythm, tempo, words, and melody. These are important as students learn to read with expression, memorize important facts, and understand concepts on a different level. Music can be used in the classroom to indicate transition times, when it is appropriate to move in an activity, as a way to calm down, and as a way to relax or energize students. Appendix C has a list of musical selections teachers might choose for different times in the instructional process.

Howard Gardner (Gardner, 1983) wrote about the eight intelligences that help us learn how we are smart. One of those intelligences is "musical." Many young people (more than many of us might realize) learn best this way. How seriously fun it would be if music were purposefully used during instruction! However, music should not be constantly playing in the classroom. Students need to have time when there is silence in the classroom, when they can think deeply without distraction and focus in on conversations. You don't want the music to become white noise. The teacher should be very intentional about deciding where and/or when music is appropriate and when it is not.

According to Chris Boyd Brewer of Johns Hopkins University, School of Education, the use of music increases the likelihood that students learn because it

- establishes a positive learning state
- creates a desired atmosphere
- builds a sense of anticipation
- energizes learning activities
- changes brain wave states
- focuses concentration
- increases attention
- improves memory
- facilitates a multisensory learning experience
- releases tension
- enhances imagination
- aligns groups
- develops rapport
- provides inspiration and motivation
- accentuates theme-oriented units
- *adds an element of fun.* (Brewer, 1995; emphasis added)

Music can accent and reinforce learning. For a classroom example, let's look at a high school health or social studies class where students are studying the 1918 Spanish influenza epidemic. Students wonder how something as ordinary as the flu affected so many people and resulted in such a high mortality rate throughout the entire world. An interesting topic becomes even more engaging when a simulation is used to visually show the spread of the disease. In this simulation, one student is designated as the virus carrier. He has a sheet of same-colored stickers. The teacher selects a music selection like "Popcorn" by Hot Butter to indicate influenza's quick spread or a funeral dirge like Bach's *Toccata*. When the music starts, students move randomly around the room. Every time the virus carrier encounters a classmate, he places a sticker on the student's hand (some students may receive more than one sticker). After sixty seconds, the music stops and students freeze. All students who have sticker(s) on their hand are counted and the number is recorded in a graph, representing the number infected over time. The infected students then remove their stickers.

In the next round, the virus carrier has a sheet of stickers for himself and three additional sheets. The music begins. The first three people the virus carrier encounters are stickered and then given their own sheet of colored dots. The three new carriers put a sticker on whomever they encounter during the sixty seconds of music. The music stops, students freeze, and all those with a sticker raise their hands. The data is recorded in a graph form. It becomes evident that the progression of the disease moves from a linear fashion (one virus carrier) to a geometric progression (multiple carriers). This simulation makes it easier for students to visualize the impact of an epidemic on a population. The music provides an oral cue and underscores the concept for learners. Although not essential to the simulation, the music helps to ensure the students will return to the information when faced later with an assessment question. If the music is intentionally selected to reinforce the concept, the students' brains are more likely to file the information in their long-term memory. The entire simulation can be found at http://www.pbs.org/wgbh/nova/education/activities/3318_02_nsn.html.

The Educator's Responsibility

Most educators are aware of the knowing-doing gap. Stanford professors Jeffery Pfeffer and Robert Sutton first coined this phrase in a book aptly titled *The Knowing-Doing Gap* (2000). The authors state that the knowing-doing gap occurs when a person empirically knows what will work and then neglects to actually put that knowledge into practice. Solid research exists and yet it is ignored, even though a specific practice has proved time and again to be beneficial. It's time to close the gap.

Research supports the positive role humor and laughter play in the classroom: students receive health benefits, both physical and emotional; are able to problem solve more effectively and retain information longer; and are more likely to be physically present. Too often, teaching professionals ignore this research and take a not-in-my-classroom attitude because they believe that there is too much content to cover and not enough time to engage in these practices. Many believe that overtly infusing fun and laughter into lesson design will take time away from valuable content and skill instruction. Others view the "messiness" as a detriment to the learning process. There is, however, much to learn from what experts, authors, practitioners, and researchers have found to be true about fun in the classroom.

The next natural step is to put these learnings into practice. To make this happen, teachers must set a goal that they will infuse fun (and maybe a little music) into their lesson planning. Based on what the research tells us, the payoff will be success for the students, immediately and in the future. When there is fun in the classroom, the students tend to persevere and work with the content and skills longer because of the climate and culture in which they are taught. Just as we would want our students to apply their learning to real-life problems, teachers should take what they know from the research and make it an integral part of their regular practice.

The chapter began with three scenarios in which most teachers might find (or have found) themselves at least once in their careers. Reflecting on how research might inform your work, you might identify at least one appropriate way to respond:

Scenario 1

Sitting in front of you is a parent whose opening statement is, "I'm not sure what you are doing. Joshua says that he has fun every day in your classroom. Fun is fine, but he's not going to be tested on fun. I'm concerned that he is not learning what he needs so that he can do well on the end-of-the-year assessment." How do you respond?

> Share with the parent the research you have and what it looks like in the classroom. Offer a specific example of how the "fun" activities in which Joshua is engaging positively impact his learning … and ultimately his test results. Then suggest that the parent ask Joshua to explain exactly what he is doing when he's having fun. If you overtly explain to your students the lesson's learning objectives—the what's, how's and why's—then students can understand

and communicate more effectively with their parents or guardians. The teacher's responsibility to explain to parents what is happening in their child's classroom has increased dramatically. And with the research supporting the effectiveness of high student engagement in learning, our efforts need to redouble.

Scenario 2

You overhear Mr. Serious loudly proclaiming to colleagues, "I don't know what is going on in that classroom. Certainly no learning. Students are up and about; she is not at the front of the room, teaching. I just know her students' scores are going to be miserable, bringing down the pass rate of the entire department. I can't wait until she is observed." How do you respond?

> This can be tricky since no one has spoken directly to you. It's probably best to wait until someone does. Mr. Serious's comments may just be a case of professional jealousy: "Her kids are having fun. I hope students don't expect that from me, because if so, they will be terribly disappointed." Often, those who are not in the know just don't know. At some point, you might want to consider politely and professionally inviting Mr. Serious into your classroom to observe a lesson. He just might turn out to be a new and helpful resource for you and, maybe, you for him!

Scenario 3

The principal asks, "Do you need more help and support this year? I notice that as I walk by there is much more noise and movement in your room than in the past. If you've got some behavior problems, maybe we can work together to get you back on the right track." How do you respond?

> It's all about the data. Ask if you can share with the principal the research you have uncovered (give her this book!) so that she can discover what you have learned. And, as in the previous scenario invite her to visit the classroom so that

your students can explain. When classroom assessment data is available, share that information with the principal to allay any doubts as to the effectiveness of your instructional choices and lesson design.

So what does the research say about serious fun? We know how much fun exists in the lives of our students outside of school; fun is their life. Much of the research that informs teaching dates back to very early in the 20th century. John Dewey once said, "Education is not preparation for life; education is life itself." Dewey's work precipitated many of the reforms and changes pervasive in classrooms today. We continually strive to learn more about what connects great teaching to successful learning. We know that effective teachers plan their lessons, pause, reflect, and incorporate the research into their teaching.

Yes, teachers should do their jobs by providing students with important learning, and students need to master that learning. But there is so much more to teaching and learning than the pervasive lecture-homework-worksheet-test model. If the learning environment is based on the research and infused with highly effective teacher behaviors, students will learn ... and learn well.

Chapter 3

How Does Serious Fun Fit into the 21st-Century Classroom?

The illiterate of the 21st century will not be those who cannot read and write, but those who cannot learn, unlearn, and relearn.

—Alvin Toffler

How can you think about incorporating serious fun into the classroom when *everyone*—the media, the PTA, the gang at the gym, the church coffee group, the board of education—is talking about how children are not adequately prepared for the 21st century? Perhaps, after all the time and effort you've invested in working on the Common Core State Standards, you may have come to the conclusion that there is no room for frivolity or fun.

It seems as though we are in a time machine. In the late 1950s and early 1960s, the interest in education was reawakened because of the pervasive belief that the United States was losing the space race with Russia. This blow to our national ego forced changes to the educational system. It became imperative for the nation's teachers to design lessons with an emphasis on mathematics and science. This shift in focus would ensure that our students would become world leaders in the development of technology. Now that we are deeply into the 21st century, the public perception is eerily the same. It seems as though helping the nation reclaim economic prosperity worldwide falls squarely on the shoulders of teachers as they prepare students for future business, college, and career opportunities. Where does a teacher legitimately find time for fun in the classroom with this burden?

Some History and Background

Before the late 1950s, education was a local and state-financed venture with curriculum and instruction locally monitored. With the launch of the Soviet satellite *Sputnik,* on October 4, 1957, the American belief that our children were the best educated in the world was shattered. The U.S. citizenry questioned whether schools in the USSR were superior to American schools and if Soviet children were better able to function in the modern world. *Sputnik* was a technological breakthrough and no one knew what would come next. "Science and technology," explained Daniel Yankelovich (1984), public opinion analyst and social scientist, "were almost universally credited with a decisive role in gaining victory in war, prosperity in peace, enhancing national security, improving our health, and enriching the quality of life." There was a pervasive feeling that graduates were not prepared to meet the challenges of modern society. Sound familiar? This possibility was not acceptable to the American people and became a wake-up call for education. The federal government reacted by passing a funding bill, the National Defense Education Act (NDEA) in 1958. The intent of the NDEA was to bring American schools at every level up to speed. Clearly, play and fun in schools were not high on the nation's agenda in the 1960s. Education was serious business; after all, the United States was behind in the space race and education was viewed as the solution for getting ahead.

Let's set the dial on our time machine to early 1961. We stand outside a typical elementary classroom. Peering through the doorway, we see thirty students sitting in desks in straight rows. The teacher's desk and a blackboard are at the front of the room. The bulk of the instruction is directed to the whole group, with the greatest importance placed on reading, writing, and mathematics. The only small-group work during the day is set aside for reading instruction. The teacher asks lots of knowledge- and comprehension-level questions, with a heavy focus on memorization of isolated facts. The teacher lectures and provides the information as students complete worksheets for reinforcement. The same scenario is played out at the high school; there's not much difference between the youngest and oldest students in how content and skill instruction is delivered. There was a call for increased graduation rates to guarantee a more educated and competitive workforce. As President Kennedy declared in his inauguration speech that year, "We shall pay any price, bear any burden, meet any hardship … to assure the survival and the success of liberty." That was the 1960s—unfortunately not so far removed from many classrooms today.

The Present and the Future of American Schools

One can see the parallels between the attitude toward education in the early 1960s and today. Concerned because American students were not performing as well as their international counterparts on assessments like the Programme for International Student Assessment (PISA) and Trends in International Mathematics and Science Study (TIMSS), the National Governors Association Center for Best Practices (NGA Center) and the Council of Chief State School Officers (CCSSO) met together in 2008 to create a plan of action. This group explored assessment results of students from fifty-seven countries on the PISA, TIMSS, and the National Assessment of Educational Progress (NAEP) in the areas of reading, writing, mathematics, and science. The top-performing countries were Finland, Hong Kong, Canada, Taiwan, Estonia, Japan, and Korea. American students were in the middle of the pack. This was unsatisfactory.

The NGA and CCSSO asked for feedback and input from stakeholders—teachers and administrators, parents, higher education and business leaders—regarding the creation of a common set of standards to be implemented across the states. The Common Core State Standards Initiative (CCSSI) developed standards differently from past reform movements. Instead of developing the standards from kindergarten and moving to the highest grade level, the Common Core State Standards (CCSS) were created from the top down. Committee members began the process by determining the desired exit outcomes for graduating students and the means to achieve them.

The Common Core is considered to be world-class, meaning that when the document was developed, the committee members identified the states and nations whose students performed best on key standardized assessments. The team members used that information to create standards with grade-level benchmarks to ensure that the outcomes are clear to all—teachers, students, parents, and the general public.

These new standards prepare students for college and career and in turn ensure that the United States is a force in the global economy. The goal of common standards across the nation is to place American students on the same playing field as students in other countries and to have consistency across states in our own country. The standards are also a response to the comments from the field that students do well in our secondary schools but are not as successful when they enter post–secondary education or the work force. Higher education and business leaders have found that students leaving high school do not have the right skill set to ensure a successful entry into higher education and/or careers. And again, just as in the 1960s, the graduation rate must improve. A highly educated citizenry is crucial for America to be a viable competitor in the global market.

The Common Core explicitly outlines "the knowledge and skills students should have within their K–12 education careers so that they will graduate from high school able to succeed in entry-level, credit-bearing academic college courses and in workforce training programs. The standards

- are aligned with college and work expectations;
- are clear, understandable and consistent;
- include rigorous content and application of knowledge through higher-order skills;
- build upon strengths and lessons of current state standards;
- are informed by other top performing countries, so that all students are prepared to succeed in our global economy and society; and
- are evidence-based." (CCSSI, 2012)

Practical Applications

Most of us would agree schools have become more accountable. The pressure has definitely been ratcheted up. We're dealing with some very serious stuff. This might manifest itself in a scenario such as this:

You're part of a team charged with incorporating the CCSS into your district's plan. You've engaged in professional development and worked hard to unpack the new core standards and compare them to what you've taught in the past. Compared to former state standards, there aren't as many concepts and skills to be taught during the year. You believe that this year you can spend more time on what is really important and maybe the students will actually understand the concepts by the close of the unit. You begin to see that the standards' focus is on critical thinking and finding relevance in the activities of daily life. You also can see that these standards are based on characteristics that 21st-century learners must have in order to survive.

According to Tony Wagner, students must possess seven survival skills:

- accessing and analyzing information
- agility and adaptability
- collaboration and leadership
- critical thinking and problem solving
- curiosity and imagination
- effective communication
- initiative (self-starting) and entrepreneurialism. (Wagner, 2008)

Upon reflection, you realize that fun just might be the vehicle that drives your students toward the destination of success called for by Wagner as well as the CCSS benchmarks. Let's delve a little deeper and see the connections between skills needed for success in the 21st century and the importance of infusing more fun, humor, laughter and play into our schools.

As you begin to design your seriously fun classroom, you consciously plan to include games in some of your lessons, either to introduce, process, or review content. As a professional, you realize that you cannot play games every day or use them as the sole way to deliver content. However, when appropriate, incorporating games into your instruction is one effective way to put an element of play and fun into the serious work of the class. Games can be an effective, rigorous way to reinforce characteristics that 21st-century learners must have to survive.

Mr. Serious Fun begins a review lesson with his high school chemistry students on the nature of solutions, precipitates, and the common ion effect. He introduces to the class a strategy referred to as the *24/7 Lecture* (Improbable Research, 2012). Mr. SF divides the class into groups of four or five students. Each group is given a topic and fifteen minutes of prep time. The task for the students is to prepare to share their assigned topic in twenty-four seconds and then conclude with a seven-word summary of the essential information. The team members are able to use their notes in their presentation and will be assessed on the accuracy of their information, their adherence to the time limit, and the specific count of words in the summary.

The teams are given their topics and the timer starts. The noise level in the room rises and falls. The teacher monitors the groups, offering help when asked. Within the teams natural leaders emerge, and they begin organizing group members to get the task completed within the time limit. Each group chooses a spokesperson to present the twenty-four seconds of information and the final summary. Competition is intense. Toward the end of the fifteen-minute preparation period, teams are practicing with timers to get as close to twenty-four seconds as possible while giving their classmates the most information they can on the topic. Wordsmiths within each group continue to fuss with the seven-word summary to get it perfect.

With just thirty seconds remaining, Mr. Serious Fun moves around the room and speaks to each group, one at a time: "Show me with your fingers how many more minutes you need." He uses this information and decides in the moment to add two more minutes. A sense of relief is evident on many faces as teams make their final push.

When it's time, Mr. Serious Fun randomly chooses one of the topics and the group with that topic is first up. The topic he chooses is *precipitation* and the group clocks in at twenty-six seconds and ends with the seven-word summary, "Emergence of a solid from a solution." The bar has been set for the remaining groups and topics. After each group shares its topic, Mr. SF asks the group's classmates if they have questions or comments on the information given. There may be a need for clarification or development of some of the responses.

Where's the match with the seven survival skills? While the students prepare their 24/7 Lectures, they first must organize their resources, notes, and ideas into a short time frame (*access and analyze information*). They *think critically* about what is essential for their peers' understanding of the chemistry topic. They work together within the group to meet the deadline (*collaborating*). Some of the group members assume a *leadership* role to better organize the team and delegate tasks. They *communicate* information with others. The team members are *creative* in arranging the material within their twenty-four-second presentation. They *adapt* their knowledge of a particular topic to fit a totally new way of presentation and, as the clock is ticking away, the students are definitely *self-starters.* Just *one* activity holds the possibility for utilizing all of the seven survival skills!

Is this just a high school phenomenon? Absolutely not. Here is a possible middle school scenario: Your students are studying the civil rights movement. Your selected objective is to have them improve their informational literacy skills with social studies content. You want your students to become more familiar with a number of significant people from the movement, such as Thurgood Marshall and Linda Brown. You assign pairs of students the seriously fun activity of creating fake Facebook pages for each assigned person. Students brainstorm the elements of a Facebook page that should be included—profile picture, cover photo, information about the person, names of the person's friends, photos, maps, timeline, and likes. After completing the necessary research using appropriate resources and citing them, the students record a set number of entries on the Facebook page, being sure to stay in character. They then download the finished file to the class's web page so that everyone can see all the Facebook pages. After the pages are completed and posted, you may assign other spin-off activities.

Compare this activity to a more traditional project in which the teacher assigns each student a person to be researched. In such an assignment, the student creates a five-page research paper and turns it in to be graded—end of assignment. If we compare the two assignments, we would find 21st-century survival skills in both, yet they would be much more prevalent in the seriously fun assignment. As an added bonus, there is a greater likelihood that the assignment will be completed and the important learning retained. The skills required for the creation of the Facebook pages are *critical thinking and problem solving* (how to best arrange and organize the page), *creativity* (the actual creation of the page), *adaptability* and *collaboration* (working with a partner, compromising), being a *self-starter* (working independently on pieces, adhering to a timeline), *effective communication,* both oral and written, and ability to *access and evaluate information* (researching and acquiring reliable and unbiased information from the Internet). Again, students are engaged in a stimulating, dynamic activity that is relevant and enjoyable. This activity fits the definition and criteria for serious fun presented in Chapter 1.

We should be thinking about consciously weaving these 21st-century survival skills into activities for students at the elementary level, as well. After all, this is and will be their world; these are their "basic" skills. In a seriously fun elementary classroom, a teacher might connect the classroom to the Library of Congress at read.gov and each day read a page or more in *The Rocket Book* by Peter Newell (Newell, 1912). Set in the early 1900s, *The Rocket Book* is the story of a rocket that is accidentally launched by the janitor's son in the basement of a twenty-story apartment building. As the rocket flies through each story, the book describes the reaction of the residents in each apartment. Read.gov includes related links to the story that are primary sources for students to examine. The story and illustrations provide an opportunity for the students to question and discuss what life was like in the beginning of the 20th century. There are new vocabulary words to discover and apply in a variety of contexts.

While reading the story, the teacher poses the question, "What if the apartment building had twenty more stories? What would happen in those apartments as the rocket swooshes up, up, and away?" In the classroom students take on the roles of editor, publisher, researcher, author, illustrator, and organizer/scheduler. Writing and illustrating the new chapters, the students *collaborate* with one another, brainstorm what might happen in each apartment (*self-starter, creativity*), access and cite illustrations to accompany the text (*access and analyze information*), take on *leadership* roles, and, of course, *communicate* effectively. When the chapters are completed with keyboarded text and illustrations and edited to everyone's satisfaction, the book is bound with a cover and shared with the larger school community. How different this process is from assigning a uniform writing prompt for all students in a language arts class! Again, the objective for both might be the same—analyzing text, improving vocabulary and writing skills, using primary documents—but the vehicle for achieving the objective is much more palatable to the students.

Serious Fun Connected to the Common Core Standards

As you review the Common Core State Standards for your grade level and content area, you'll discover rich opportunities to put into place fun activities that reach the same objectives as you might find with a standard same-old, same-old assignment. You can do this without taking time away from your students learning content or skills or burdening yourself with four or five *more* hours of prep each week.

The CCSSI calls for higher-order thinking skills to be embedded in the teaching and learning that occurs at all levels. The bar has been raised. In addition, reasoning, communication, collaboration, and the use of information and technology literacy are competencies that are to be integrated in the content areas. Although there may be a place for worksheets, a steady diet of students working on worksheets is no longer a model of good teaching.

As you unpack the CCSS in mathematics, you realize that the eight Standards for Mathematical Practices (SMP) stress 21st-century skills. In the P21 Common Core Toolkit, the mathematical practices can be categorized under critical thinking and problem solving, communication and information literacy.

SMP #1 asks that students "make sense of problems and persevere in solving them." When students are engaged and involved in activities that are fun, they tend to have a higher degree of stick-to-it-ness. Teaching students to be mathematicians and mess around with math can be done more easily when they are involved in a game or a puzzle that intrigues them or is relevant in some way to them. Often in those situations students do not get the answer quickly but are so involved that time passes by as they are thinking about possible solutions. They are in the flow of the problem (Csikszentmihalyi & Csikszentmihalyi, 1988, p. 323). Contrast that situation to one where a student solves a number of isolated, knowledge-level problems on a worksheet. You may have watched a student struggle with these problems for a short time, throw up his hands in frustration, and give up. He is discouraged and doesn't see an end in sight. The student is not motivated to continue so the teacher helps him, encourages him, coddles him, and, as a result, unwittingly builds a sense of learned helplessness in the student. In contrast, when we present content in unique, engaging, and fun ways, we pique students' interest and curiosity, opening the door to learning. We encourage them to persevere.

An example of a mathematical concept that students need to learn is how to find a percentage of increase or decrease. One way for a teacher to present this lesson is to have the student complete a worksheet with a series of problems like "What is 458 increased by 7%?" (CCSS: Math.6.RP.3c). Another way—using the same concept, percentage of increase—is to tell students that they are going shopping. Each student is given a set amount of hypothetical money, $500, and told to spend, spend, spend. They must use flyers and catalogs or access websites to purchase goods. They generate a list of items that includes prices, remembering to add in the local sales tax of 7%. Finally, a subtotal is calculated to be sure they stay within their $500 budget. The same content is now infused with an element of choice and fun. With this activity, students persevere to find the correct answer. At the core of this activity is a problem in which the content is presented in an atypical way and is relevant to the student's life.

In the CCSS for English Language Arts, fourth-grade students are asked to develop, implement, and communicate new ideas to others through original writing using technology (CCSS: ELA.W.4.3, 4.6). A standard assignment is to have students read a familiar piece of poetry that is included in the Grade 4–5 Text Exemplars (CCSS, Appendix B), like "The New Colossus" by Emma Lazarus. Students then respond in writing to the prompt, "If you were an immigrant, what would the Statue of Liberty symbolize for you?" The students keyboard their three-paragraph response or create a six-slide PowerPoint with each slide having no more than four bullets, one illustration, and one transition.

Contrast this with an activity in a seriously fun classroom. As a large group, students read and discuss the poem "The New Colossus." Using appropriate resources, students then research images of immigrants who entered the United States through Ellis Island in the early 1900s and learn how to evaluate the sources to be sure that they are nonbiased and true. Students are then grouped into teams of two. Each pair selects an image of a specific immigrant at Ellis Island. Working together, the students prepare a character study of the person in the photo. The pair develops a script for a radio broadcast with one of the students assuming the role of a reporter and the other representing the immigrant. They create a podcast of the interview that is shared on the class website. This learning is interdisciplinary, uses technology, allows the student autonomy and choice, and reinforces several of the 21st-century skills.

The CCSS Reading and Writing Standards are not just for English class. The intention is for teachers of all subject areas to incorporate the Reading and Writing Standards into their specific content. So teachers of history and social studies, science and technical subjects cannot heave a sigh of relief and think they are off the hook. Many content-specific trained teachers feel uncomfortable considering how to incorporate the literacy pieces into their instruction, let alone in a seriously fun way. How can teachers do this? Let's take a look at a high school physics example.

In the CCSS at Grade 11–12 under the anchor standard *Writing, Text Types and Purposes,* students are expected to write arguments focused on discipline-specific content. They must develop precise claims, examine counterclaims, and logically defend the claim with supporting evidence (CCSS: WHST.11.1a, 1b). This sounds like a daunting task that is difficult to imagine as fun, but with a little preparation and thought, it can be done—seriously.

The following lesson, based on the ideas of Lori Stewart (2012), is tied to multiple literacy and mathematics standards. To begin, the teacher uses a generic review activity to go over the vocabulary that will be in the lesson. In this unit of study, the prerequisite terms are "speed," "acceleration," "momentum," "Newton's Laws of Motion," "gravity," and "free-fall." This vocabulary exploration taps into the CCSS Reading Standards for Literacy in Science and Technical Subjects, Grade 11–12: Craft and Structure.

Once the teacher is sure that the students understand the vocabulary and the formulas that are relevant to the task, the next step is for students to defend or dispute the claim that in popular media the laws of physics are frequently exaggerated or broken. The teacher gathers a number of Wile E. Coyote and Roadrunner cartoons. These are readily available on YouTube. What student wouldn't want to watch cartoons in school?!

The students watch the clips from YouTube, stop watch in hand. Odds are that in any Wile E. Coyote cartoon he will take a tumble off a cliff. Students watch the cartoon and time how long it takes him to hit the ground. They time the fall at 6 seconds. The formula students use to calculate the height of the cliff is "distance equals one half times gravity times time squared." For this example their equation will be d = ½ ($9.8 \text{ m/s}^2 \times 6^2$s). Students will soon discover that Wile E. Coyote just fell off a 176-meter cliff (roughly 600 feet, a 60-story drop!) and walked away ready to do battle with the Roadrunner another day (Stewart, 2012). A very seriously fun extension would be to have students perform the same task as if Wile E. was on another planet. Students determine which variables would change and what the outcome might be for him.

After solving the equation, the students go back to their original claim that cartoons (or action films or fantasy shows) do or do not ignore the laws of physics. They write their claim, sequence their data and evidence to support their claim, and state their conclusion. As a culminating activity, the students share their snippet of cartoon with other groups in the classroom and summarize their claim, including proof to support it. It's a classroom version of Mythbusters. We have just had a seriously fun activity in an upper-secondary science class that focuses on multiple standards in the Common Core. It can be done!

We identified 21st-century survival skills for the activities mentioned earlier in the chapter. The first activity was the 24/7 Lecture, a strategy used in a high school chemistry class. In the CCSS, the content is found in Reading Standards for Literacy in Science and Technical Subjects. Key Ideas and Details, #2: "Determine the central ideas or conclusions of a text."

The teacher's objective for the students as they created Facebook pages for notable people from the civil rights movement is contained in the CCSS in Reading Standards for Literacy in History/Social Studies, Key Ideas and Details, #1: "Cite specific textual evidence to support analysis"; #7: "Interpret visual information"; #8: "Distinguish among fact, opinion and reasoned judgment in a text"; and #9: "Analyze the relationship between a primary and secondary source on the same topic."

The activity with *The Rocket Book* targets multiple standards, domains, and clusters, making it a perfect strategy to use if you are looking to focus on multiple standards in one activity.

The Change Process

Any time we are asked to face change, it is a challenge, especially in education. Change is the only thing in our lives that will remain constant; we *always* have to be ready to change. Transitioning our educational practices from the 20th century to the 21st is a daunting challenge, one which we must continue to pursue in order to see success. However, as you change and adapt, it makes no sense to throw the baby out with the bathwater. So much of your current success is due to the hard work to which you have been committed from the beginning of your career.

Since you have read this far, you certainly have a goal of creating a seriously fun classroom (or, more likely, a *more* seriously fun classroom). How do you navigate this transition and survive with your professional sanity intact? Consider these points as you review your lessons:

- Reflect. How did the lesson go when you used it previously?
- Think about reviewing and tweaking your current lessons. What pieces of the lessons worked? How are they already seriously fun?
- Align the objectives for the lessons with the CCSS or state or local standards.
- Label the 21st-century skills that are currently included in each of the lessons. Are there more that can be included seamlessly?
- Inquire. Is there a way to make the learning more relevant or real-world for the student?

It's important to note that Mr. Serious Fun wasn't always as successful as he is now. He struggled early, trying to make his classroom environment more seriously fun by infusing humor and engaging his students in strategies he was convinced would work. Every now and then he failed, sometimes miserably. One of the first times he "changed things up a little," he tried a strategy called *Snowball Review*. He had students write down one important piece of content on different colored sheets of paper. They crumpled the papers into balls (snowballs). On his signal, he gave them two minutes to throw the snowballs around the room. After the two minutes was up, his plan was to have students retrieve a snowball of a different color than the one they had written on, partner up, and take turns reading the information and reacting with their partners. To say that pandemonium reigned is putting it mildly. He knew after just one minute of snowball fighting that the strategy was causing too much extended chaos.

That evening at home, Mr. SF took the time to reflect and analyze. "What went wrong and what can I do about it?" he asked himself. He decided to adapt *Snowball Review* by allowing his students only thirty seconds for their snowball fight. He waited a couple of weeks before trying it out. This time it worked much better but was still not as effective as he would have liked. He added an assessment piece the third time he tried it by collecting the papers after students had responded with their partners. That evening he read through the comments and decided that students had a strong grasp of the content and he could move on to the next concept. Mr. Serious Fun continued in this same fashion year after year, deliberately adding seriously fun activities to his instruction until his classroom became a place students really wanted to be ... every day!

Thinking back on the five points posed earlier, let's get into the brain of Mr. Serious Fun. Let's discover how he used them to improve his teaching as he continued on his mission of making his classroom more seriously fun.

- The impetus for using the *Snowball Review* strategy was a result of reflection upon a lesson he'd used previously. In the past, he had his students participate in "relay races" to the board. The main thing he realized was that 100 percent of his students were not actively participating. The races had a small degree of fun, but Mr. SF wanted more.

- By trying *Snowball Review*, he kept the kinesthetics inherent in the relay races and increased the level of overt active participation by all students, which made the activity novel and more fun.

- The CCSS was fundamental in the content his students were reviewing. He honestly felt he could tie every important piece of content students wrote on their papers to a standard, domain, and/or cluster.

- In designing *Snowball Review,* Mr. SF identified up front the 21st-century skills. He was more confident that he was adequately preparing his students for their futures when they collaborated, a skill he believes is of vital importance.

- Mr. Serious Fun knew that throwing snowballs was not a real-world application of learned content. He did recognize, however, that when students get out of their seats, move around, laugh a little, and work with classmates, each child is certainly engaged in behaviors that will be an essential part of their adult lives. Mr. SF was purposeful and intentional in including movement in the activity.

So how does serious fun fit into the 21st-century classroom? You want your students to know that your classroom is not the same as their grandmother's classroom. You break away from the 1960s by *thinking critically* as you *create* lessons that are integral to a good education. You work through the challenges that are inherent in change and engage in complex *problem solving.* Searching through your files, you discover some great lessons that need a little (or a lot) of *adapting.* There is usually a colleague nearby with whom you can work *collaboratively.* Yet there will be times when you have to go it alone. Be confident in your own ability to *start the work by yourself.* You possess the skills that allow you to design seriously fun activities. Make sure everyone knows what you're doing. *Communicate* clearly and frequently with students, parents, colleagues, administrators, and the community at large. And, at the end of the day, take that crucial time to be reflective. Ask yourself how things went. *Evaluate* your success and be prepared to make changes as you forge onward.

Your charge is to prepare students for future success through the use of fun in the learning environment. Theodore Roosevelt said, "The best thing you can do is the right thing; the next best thing you can do is the wrong thing; the worst thing you can do is nothing." Start today by implementing at least one new strategy that encourages fun and laughter in your classroom. By modeling risk-taking for your students, you will teach them a life lesson that it is good to take calculated risks once in a while because the rewards can be high. When you work hard to achieve your goal to improve the learning environment, everyone connected to that environment benefits. You'll find that having a seriously fun classroom is the best thing to happen to you as an educator.

Chapter 4

How Do I Bring Serious Fun into My Classroom?

Play gives children a chance to practice what they're learning.

—Mr. Fred Rogers

You're already acquainted with one of our teachers, Mr. Serious Fun. Let's look again at one of his classes.

It's early in the school year as Mr. SF stands at his classroom door, smiling and welcoming his class of twenty-seven fourth graders. One by one, they file past, shoulders slumped. They look at the daily agenda and see that math is first on the docket for today. "Not math—I hate math!" says one particularly sullen boy. He and his classmates reluctantly move to their seats. Some heads immediately plop down on desks. Given that it is 8:30 in the morning, you might think these children would be awake and raring to go. That, obviously, is not the case.

Attendance is taken and administrivia dealt with. A few minutes later, Mr. SF asks for the class's attention. He fires up the projector and shows a cartoon about how a snow day had closed school on the day of a test. A few snickers ripple through the students. Next, Mr. SF utters a dreadful phrase: "To get you excited about next week's test on geometry ..." The groans return. He waits patiently for them to die down and finishes: "... we'll do some review. And I have something a little different. Actually, it might be a *lot* different from what you are used to doing, and I think you're going to like it." This comment brings a couple of heads off the desks. Curiosity is starting to get the best of some of these nine- and ten-year-olds.

"How many of you have ever played Bingo?" the teacher asks. A stray hand or two rises in the air. Some of those hands go about halfway, propped up at the elbow by the other hand.

"Well, today, we're going to play a little Bingo of our own: Human Bingo." Heads rotate to catch what is happening. Novelty and inquisitiveness are taking over and Mr. Serious Fun is starting to "turn" his class. "Maybe class won't be so bad, after all," we hear from the child who was so gloomy just a few minutes ago.

Mr. SF distributes a handout to students that looks a lot like a Bingo board: nine boxes arranged in a 3 × 3 configuration. A "FREE SPACE" occupies the center box. In the other boxes are short phrases or questions, such as "Can describe something with line symmetry" and "Can define a right triangle." Upon further inspection, students notice that some boxes have fun phrases, like "Will sing part of a favorite song."

Will share a favorite hobby	Knows how many degrees are in a circle	Can define a right triangle
Will sing part of a favorite song	**FREE SPACE!**	Will make a funny sound
Can describe something with line symmetry	Will identify the properties shared by squares and rectangles	Knows the number of sides on a pentagon

Mr. SF continues: "Now that you each have a handout, it's time to explain exactly how this game works. Everyone ready?" He notices a sea of nods and quite a few smiles. Most of the students seem eager to learn more and get moving so he moves on to the slides with the directions and rules of the game.

"The entire class has five minutes and twenty-three seconds to move around the room and visit eight *different* classmates. Each time you connect with someone, ask them to respond to one of the boxes on your Human Bingo board. If they answer the question correctly, write that person's name in the appropriate box. If not, say 'Thanks' and move on to someone else. You must have classmates answer *all* the prompts *correctly*. By the end of the time, you will have eight different names, one in each of the eight boxes. Once your board is filled, please return to your seat." After modeling this, he asks, "How can I clarify this first part of Human Bingo?"

There are a few questions and the teacher does his best to clear them up. He starts a piece of music designed to get his students up and moving, maybe even dancing a little, starts the timer, and shouts "Go!" Given the short time allotted to fill their boards, students spring out of their seats and begin to search out classmates for right answers.

As the time expires, most students have returned to their seats. Mr. Serious Fun assists a few of them, even letting them write *his* name in a few boxes.

"OK. Now on to Part 2," he says. "Here's a jar full of popsicle sticks with all of our names on them. Different people will choose one name at random from the jar. As a name is called, check your Human Bingo card. If you have that name in *one* of the boxes, place a colored chip in the box." Mr. SF models this for students. "Once you get three in a row, horizontally, vertically, or diagonally, rise out of your seat and exclaim joyously: 'Human Bingo!'"

Students take turns removing popsicle sticks from the jar. After the sixth name, Susan rises out of her seat and cries, "Human Bingo!" "Great!" says Mr. SF, "but hold on. There is one more part to our activity. Susan will read each of the three boxes in her line and the name of each person in each of the boxes. In order for her to win, each of those three people must give the correct answers to each prompt." Susan gets all three of them to respond correctly and thus becomes the winner of Human Bingo. The class then works in pairs for the next few minutes discussing the correct responses to all of the geometry-related prompts. A couple of students need clarification, which they get from classmates and Mr. Serious Fun.

Needless to say, the students had fun. They were also engaged. And they learned (or reviewed) some geometry. The activity was filled with academic rigor in that most of the prompts were content-related to the upcoming test. But Mr. SF also was determined to honor the reality that his students are very social beings so he provided prompts that allowed an "outlet" for socialization (Havighurst and Davis, 1943). As he moved around the room, pausing at different groups of students, Mr. Serious Fun was able to formatively assess his students' knowledge of the content. He made notes and collected his thoughts in writing so that he could refer to them later.

Making Fun an Instructional Priority

Early in this book, you were asked, "Why should I infuse fun into school?" While it might have appeared to be a rhetorical question, this *reflective* question is essential to any well-planned, quality lesson delivered in any classroom anywhere at any time. An important part of a successful lesson is the decision making the teacher undertakes in order to successfully facilitate learning. Madeline Hunter, one of the first educators to recognize the importance of instructional theory, said that teachers make decisions that "consciously and deliberately" increase their students' learning (Hunter, 1982, p. 6). Dr. Hunter's instructional elements and strategies are essential if teachers are to bring content to life for their students.

We examined 21st-century skills earlier. And if it's true that serious fun promotes creativity, problem solving, application of knowledge to real life, collaboration, and good communication, then it should be imperative to infuse more fun into the learning environment.

As you make the instructional decision as to which strategy to use, it will be important to understand the distinction between productive fun and pointless frivolity. We can't say frequently enough that schools are places of seriously hard work. They are not to be converted into playgrounds where academics take a back seat. Not everything that happens in the classroom will have an overt component of laughter, fun, play, or humor. Ultimate and real success is all about motivating students and engaging them in their learning. Our belief is that this can happen more readily when we *do* laugh and/or play. Some of the strategies in this book simply provide a more engaging alternative to "Write this in your notes," "Think about this," or "Turn to your neighbor and discuss this." Yet the element of fun, as we have seen repeatedly, can have enormous benefits.

Assessment Possibilities

The definition of serious fun offered in Chapter 1 includes two significant words: "academics" and "rigorous." There are multiple opportunities for assessment in a seriously fun classroom. It's important for teachers to pay careful attention to what students are learning and be sure that learning is rigorous. Many teachers will be excited to infuse fun and humor into their work *and*, at the same time, discover what their students are and possibly aren't learning. The assessments put forth in *Serious Fun* are primarily formative in nature. This includes the informal and sometimes formal activities that teachers use as they monitor student learning during instruction and make the necessary adjustments to their teaching. When students are actively engaged in their learning, it is critical for planning to know if the intended learning is indeed occurring. Formative assessment can be qualitative and quantitative but is seldom used to evaluate students (assign grades). Instead, it provides feedback for teachers as they plan for future lessons.

Seriously Fun Strategies

There are nearly seventy strategies throughout this book. That's a lot, which is a good thing; the more choices there are, the more likely you will find strategies that work for your particular class. To make the search for successful strategies more attainable, they have been categorized as follows:

- **Chapter 5:** *Getting Ready to Learn.* This chapter describes strategies that set the stage, prepare students for what's coming, access prior knowledge, etc.

- **Chapter 6:** *Class-Building and Team-Building.* This chapter describes strategies in which students learn to work with classmates successfully, allowing them to focus on collaboration, one of the critical 21st-century survival skills.

- **Chapter 7:** *Processing Content.* This chapter describes strategies that allow students to practice, prepare, and work with new learning.

- **Chapter 8:** *Movement.* This chapter describes strategies that energize the body and the brain and give students the chance to expend a little energy.

- **Chapter 9:** *Closure.* This chapter describes strategies that give the brain a chance to pause and reflect, thus improving long-term retention of content and skills.

- **Chapter 10** has a number of content-specific activities that target directly a specified content area (chemistry, economics, algebra, etc.).

The reader might notice that these chapters are titled and ordered to reflect some of the components of good lesson design: get the brain ready to learn, have students work with others, practice and process new learning, find opportunities for movement, and provide closure. It's entirely possible and maybe even preferable to choose one strategy from each chapter and incorporate them into a single class period. Fun and learning will be high on the agenda *that* day!

Appendix D contains three sample lessons, one at each grade-cluster level, that are built around the essential elements of instruction and adhere to good lesson design. Each is tied to specific, national standards and 21st-century skills, begins with a learning objective, and uses seriously fun strategies. Classrooms are too unique and diverse for this book to provide the specificity needed for individual lessons. Teachers know their own standards, learning objectives, goals, and students best.

So how exactly do you bring serious fun into your classroom? Continue reading. Skip around from chapter to chapter, reading different sections of this book. Perhaps you're looking for something specific. When you do find an idea you like, make a note, preferably written rather than mental. This gives you that all-important opportunity for reflection, which is necessary for growth. Then, when you're ready, pick up the book again. Search for even more seriously fun ideas. They're waiting for you ... and so are your students.

Chapter 5

Seriously Fun Strategies for Getting Ready to Learn

So long as there's a bit of a laugh going, things are all right.

—D. H. Lawrence

Much of what we know today about preparing the brain and the body for learning comes from the work of Madeline Hunter. Dr. Hunter coined the phrase "anticipatory set": by anticipating what is about to come, the brain gets set for learning (Hunter, 1982, p. 27). Just as someone exercising the body warms up first, students need to warm up before exercising the brain so that new learning that is introduced sticks ... and stays.

It's not just Dr. Hunter. Multiple studies have proven time and time again that accessing background or prior knowledge is powerful in priming the learning (Marzano, 2004). Retrieving or providing background knowledge can go a long way to get students ready and motivated to learn. When students' brains are primed and set to learn, the likelihood of mastery and retention increases dramatically. Teachers should consider the critical attributes of an anticipatory set when planning lessons for students: involve *all* learners, connect the new learning to something relevant, and create a congruent bridge to the learning (Hunter, 1982). An anticipatory set to learning works best if it's "thought provoking, interesting, *fun*, or exciting" (Colorado

Department of Education, 2010; emphasis added). If we can properly ready students for learning, then maybe that learning will become as permanent as concrete.

Ready, set, go!

Classroom Contest

Based on the TV show *Family Feud*, *Classroom Contest* engages learners as they compete against each other to see who can come up with the most ideas. The teacher begins by posing a content-related prompt. Students work alone or in small groups, generating possible responses. For example, in a psychology class, the students have been exploring multiple intelligences. They are asked to think of possible responses to the question, "What are some reasons to learn about multiple intelligences?" The teacher lists ten (or any other number that is appropriate) "right answers" (important learnings/points/ ideas that pertain to the material being studied) in reverse order, from 10 to 1. Number 1 in the psychology example might be "Make learning engaging and exciting for all!"

Points are awarded each time students offer a response that matches the ones shared by the teacher. Students keep track of points scored and a winner is declared. To add a level of academic rigor and a little twist to the game, have students lobby for responses they had that the teacher did not. The teacher or, better yet, classmates can decide if those responses are worthy, and double points can be awarded.

Consensogram

A *Consensogram* is an instructional strategy that generates data about student opinions, attitudes, or knowledge about a specific issue or piece of content. It is gathered and presented in a large visual format, resembling a bar graph. It's interactive and kinesthetic, offering ample opportunity for conversation and perhaps a little fun.

Begin by choosing an issue or topic. In a social studies class, the topic might be the United States' role as a global peacekeeper. Write the statement at the top of a large sheet of chart paper. The next task is to decide on the items to place along the horizontal axis at the bottom. In this example, the choices include a range of roles: "Hands Off," "Minimally Involved," "Some Involvement," "Fully Engaged."

U.S. Role as a Global Peacekeeper Should Be

| Hands Off | Minimally involved | Some involvement | Fully Engaged |

Students each take one sticky note and place it above the role they think the United States should take. Students stack their notes vertically up the chart paper, creating a bar graph. Once the *Consensogram* is complete, it's time to talk about the information displayed. Ask students to explain where they placed their sticky note and why. A general class conversation is likely to ensue, and, depending on the nature of the topic, issue, or prompt, the conversation could be quite lively.

Keep the *Consensogram* conspicuously posted in the classroom as the unit progresses. If appropriate, revisit the question at the end of the unit to see if there has been a shift in beliefs. Reflection on the learning can be greatly enhanced by using the *Consensogram* as a reference.

Defend or Dispute

Defend or Dispute can be an extremely spirited way to begin a lesson. A family and consumer science teacher might make a statement that requires a judgment, like "A sales tax on sugary beverages will reduce obesity." Ask students to choose a side: defend the statement or dispute it and offer sound reasons for the stance taken. Pair up opposing students and have them engage in conversation. In order to hold students accountable for listening with an open mind, students must share one thing their opponent said that might make them reconsider their original stance.

A variation can be to randomly assign students to defend and dispute a piece of content. If it is something that is pretty much indisputable, it can be very good (and possibly a little fun) practice for students to actually find a way to make a case for disputing the statement. Be sure to balance the opportunities for students to work on both sides of the argument.

First Word

Any unit of study, whether ten minutes or a full class period, can begin with *First Word*. The topic or term to be summarized becomes an acronym. Students brainstorm all the things they already know about the topic and then elaborate on those ideas to create words and/or phrases that start with each of the letters of the topic. In an art history class about cubism, the students create words and/or phrases that start with *C*, *U*, *B*, *I*, *S* and *M*. The resulting lists can be used by the teacher as an excellent assessment tool for planning purposes.

Let's Get Ready to … LEARN!

Let's Get Ready to … LEARN! is based on the KWL strategy created by Donna Ogle (Ogle, 1986). A teacher in an English language arts class might begin with the following: "For our upcoming unit of study next week on how to analyze an author's voice, I have prepared lessons with activities to focus your learning. But I'm curious to hear what *you* have to say. Your task for the weekend is to take a few moments and think about how you would respond to these two prompts:

1. What do you already KNOW about author's voice?
2. What do you WANT to learn about author's voice?"

When the next class convenes, students can work in whatever fashion the teacher decides. They share what they already KNOW with each other and note what they WANT to learn.

Spend a Buck

Spend a Buck is a decision-making strategy that gives students the opportunity to prioritize choices. Students are offered choices and understand that it is OK to have differing opinions about a topic. The teacher gives each student an equal amount of play money—say, five $1 bills. The teacher then announces a number of different options: homework problems to go over, homework problems to be assigned, different statements about content, or options about what comes next. The possibilities are almost endless. The choices are then physically displayed around the room or projected on a screen. Students "spend" their "bucks" by committing a certain amount of money to the choices. For example, an economics teacher is planning to have her students explore the reasons for the United States' most recent recession. She lists three reasons for students to consider. One student might want to spend two dollars on one choice, three on another, and none on the third. Another student puts all five of his bucks on one choice because he really wants to study that one. The totals for each choice (how much money was spent) are calculated. The most popular choice is the selection on which students spent the most money. This is where the teacher begins instruction.

Two Truths and a Fib

Two wrongs don't make a right … but what about two rights and a wrong? Either way, *Two Truths and a Fib* is a strategy that is very easy to use, academically rigorous, and can surely make for a lot of fun.

To use *Two Truths* as a team-builder, the teacher begins by preparing three statements about himself or herself: two that are true and one that is a fib. Make the three statements a little tricky. For example, one of this book's authors might use these three statements: "Born in Mississippi," "Had ten different jobs before becoming a teacher," and "Has written music and recorded a CD." It's up to the class to separate the facts from fiction. Turn this exercise into 20 Questions and have students sleuth to identify the fib.

For a content-related variation, present students with three statements related to material being studied, two true and one not. Students can work individually or collaboratively. The teacher circulates around the room as students work to uncover the fib. A health teacher whose class is studying HIV/AIDS might start with these three statements: "HIV stands for human immune virus," "The term AIDS applies to the most advanced stages of HIV infection," and "HIV is found in bodily fluids of a person who has been infected."

As an extension to the lesson or as an assessment, assign "homeplay" to the class. Students create two truths and one fib about the lesson's content. The next day, volunteers can try to stump their classmates by presenting their three statements. Truthfully, and this is no fib, a good time will be had by all.

Vanity Me

Even if students are too young to drive, they still will enjoy this activity. Photocopy a license plate and then cover up the numbers and/or letters, leaving a blank rectangular space in the center. Images might

also be found on the web. Enlarge the icon so that it is about the same size as a real license plate. Two plates will fit on one 8½ × 11 sheet of paper, used the long ("hot dog") way.

Students create their very own vanity plate to hang from their "vehicle" (desk or chair). Although most states limit the number and type of characters allowed, teachers can choose to follow this rule or not use any limitations at all, other than, of course, proper and respectful language.

As an example, students in a history class could be assigned a historical figure, like Abraham Lincoln. What might his vanity plate have looked like? "Unify," "1st Republican," and "Log Splitter" are possibilities.

Chapter 6

Seriously Fun Strategies for Class-Building and Team-Building

When people laugh together, they cease to be young and old, master and pupils, workers and drivers. . . . They become a single group of human beings enjoying its existence.

—Gilbert Highet

The old adage that "two heads are better than one" has its place in our schools. The research presented on 21st-century learning emphasizes a number of skills vital to success. One of them, collaboration, emphasizes the importance of working together.

Class-building strategies focus primarily on developing a cohesive classroom. However, there are practitioners who feel the focus in our classrooms should only be on content. It's vital for us to seriously consider what we believe the focus of schools should be. What do we want from the 21st-century learners in our classrooms? Is it primarily a solid command of basic facts such as memorizing formulas for area, reciting dates of famous battles, diagramming sentences, or remembering the periodic table? Or do we want a more balanced approach for our students, by which we intentionally provide opportunities for them to attain those 21st-century skills and become productive members of an effective team?

Class-building activities are used when it's important for students to collaborate and work together as an *entire* class. This is done in an ongoing, deliberate fashion to build camaraderie. Depending on the learning objective, the strategies and activities can have an academic focus or not. A combination of content and fun is preferable most of the time.

Team-building strategies and activities can take place frequently, perhaps a few times each week. Some team-builders incorporate questions to help individuals learn more about their teammates. The objective of this type of team-builder is to create higher levels of trust between team members and increase support for one another. Another way to build teams in classrooms is to relate the team's outcome to the content being studied. Structures must be in place so that everyone is involved, engaged, and held accountable. Social skills and reflection are also necessary as effective teams are evidence of a class's behavior.

One of the benefits of collaboration as an entire class and/or team is efficiency, something educators strive for every day. When people work together, there is less for each individual member to accomplish and goals are more quickly attained. Needing smaller amounts of time to complete the team's goal (and a little less brain power) places less stress on individual students.

Another benefit of students working with their classmates is the identification of unique skills of individual members that enable teams to be more effective and efficient. Diverse strengths are combined, bringing about an improved final product and an increase in creativity. In terms of interpersonal skills, two of the critical 21st-century skills, listening and good communication, are integral to the class's and/or team's success.

Perhaps the biggest advantage in taking valuable class time to have students work collaboratively is that relationships strengthen and the parts become a unified whole. Relationships can be the decisive factor to success in our schools. Establishing strong bonds between student and teacher or between classmates allows the brain to be more open to exploration, discovery, and retention of material. And when students have the chance to meet, greet, and sit with classmates, they become more engaged in their learning. Whether the purpose is for academics or fun, there is no doubt that when students work together to reach a common goal, they'll be more engaged (and successful) in their learning.

Block Out

Block Out is a strategy that can begin or end a unit. Organize students into groups of two or three. Distribute a sheet of paper with a 2 × 3 table. In each space write a different prompt, with most but not all of them related to the topic being explored. Be sure to choose a prompt or two that is fun. Then cover each block with a small sticky note.

Below is an example from a unit on "writ[ing] arguments focused on *discipline-specific content*" (CCSS: WHST.6.1) in Grade 6:

What is meant by using "logical reasoning" when one is making a claim?	Share a good word to use when trying to support a claim you have made.
What exciting plans do you have for the weekend?	Why is it important to have a strong concluding statement in your argument?
How might you use what we have been learning in your life?	Vividly describe your favorite food.

The student who begins (see *For the Role of . . .* later in this chapter) removes one of the sticky notes and reads the statement that appears. She shares her response to the prompt with the group. The paper is then passed to the next person, moving in a clockwise direction. The process repeats itself until all prompts have been uncovered, allowing each person to participate more than once. During this activity, the teacher moves from group to group, listening to the responses, formatively assessing students, and making mental or written notes about any misconceptions, areas to reinforce, or points to be emphasized with the entire class. The teacher can then ask students to share what they heard or learned or what might need additional clarification.

Color-Coding

As a way to form teams, distribute colored index cards or place small, colored stickers on handouts and worksheets. Call on students with a specific color to answer questions. As an example, those with yellow cards are to answer Question #1, blue cards, Question #2, and so on. Teachers can also assign colors to questions ahead of time to allow students to generate responses for their specific question.

The distribution of color-coded cards can be an intentional way of differentiating instruction. Questions corresponding to different colors might be written at varying levels. For example, yellow cards could be literal-level questions; green cards, analytical; and blue cards, comprehension questions.

After allowing groups of students to work on their particular questions, the colors could be combined so that each student is exposed to all of the questions.

Exquisite Corpse

Exquisite Corpse, based on a parlor game invented by surrealism's principal founder, André Breton, in the 1920s, can have huge implications for making learning more engaging and fun. It's described as a "progressive story game." Originally, *Exquisite Corpse* was played by several people, each of whom would write a phrase on a sheet of paper, fold the paper to conceal that part of it, and pass it on to the next player for an additional contribution.

Arrange students into groups of three or four. Each team is given one sheet of 8½ × 11 paper, folded into sixths or eighths. Player One begins by writing a piece of relevant content—a word, phrase, sentence, drawing, illustration, and so on—in the top section of the paper. He hands the paper to the person to his left. She looks at the first entry and writes a comment on what she sees in the second section. She folds the first, top section under so that it is concealed from view.

The second player then passes the paper to the third person. Each time, the person receiving the paper sees only *one* section (the previous one), makes a new entry, and then folds the previous entry under and out of sight. This process continues until each student has responded twice. When the third or fourth person has responded for the second time, the paper is completely unfolded and entries are compared, especially the first and last. An option is to have students alternate between linguistic (words and/or phrases) and nonlinguistic (illustrations) representations.

For example, in a math class, the first person might write "A = lw." The second person might draw a rectangle. The third person, who sees *only* that drawing, might recognize it as something shaped like a rectangle and write "sheet of paper." Person Four sees *only* "sheet of paper" and responds accordingly.

An English language arts teacher could have the students write a progressive story. Each student adds to the plot by reacting *only* to the preceding statement.

Find Someone Who/People Search/ Treasure Hunt

When it's time for students (or adults) to gather information from a number of different people, this is a strategy that will do just that. Participants search for information about their colleagues or about a subject matter ... or, better yet, both.

Find Someone Who is engaging for learners of all ages because it gives them the chance to get up, move around, and connect with each another. For example, it is an excellent way to begin a faculty meeting. Before the meeting, the principal prepares a handout with a list of search requirements. They are a mix of prompts related to the meeting's topic and a few just for fun. When the signal is given or a piece of music is started, folks move around the room, connecting with others. The sample below has four statements, three of which are content-related. For example, Taylor takes her paper and meets Kendell. Taylor asks Kendell which of the squares she can complete. Kendell offers "Obtained a degree from an out-of-state college/university." Taylor writes "Kendell" in that space. Kendell returns the favor for Taylor. As soon as each person has found the required number of responses (four to six is a good range to use), they return to their seats, ready to begin the meeting.

_____ spent the past summer working with the
    Name   Common Core.

_____ obtained a degree from an out-of-state college or
    Name   university.

_____ knows the location of emergency substitute plans.
    Name

_____ can give a reason for incorporating serious fun into
    Name   our work.

In the classroom setting, deciding what to do with the completed sheets is a teacher choice. One suggestion is to have students who filled in content-related boxes explain their responses. An example list for an economics class is displayed on page 62. In this example, the combination of content-related and fun items allows this activity to maintain academic rigor while also honoring people's need to socialize by letting them talk with each other.

_____ knows what the BLS is.
Name

_____ has seen a really great movie lately.
Name

_____ can briefly explain how unemployment insurance
Name   works.

_____ will define what is meant by a "business cycle."
Name

For the Role of ...

It can be advantageous for classroom management to have clearly defined roles when working collaboratively in pairs or small groups. These could be roles like who goes first or next, who collects materials, who records information, and so on. There are lots of fun ways to assign roles.

For example, the teacher could ask which member of the class

- was born the farthest away?
- sits at the desk farthest from the door/teacher's desk/window?
- has the darkest/lightest hair?
- has the most/least buttons on his/her clothing?
- has the most/least/largest/smallest pockets?
- has a birthday closest to or farthest from today?
- has a phone number that gives the greatest/smallest sum when of all the digits are added together?
- has the most/least number of letters in both first and last names?
- is wearing the most of a specific color?
- has the darkest/lightest eyes?

To infuse some surprise into this, especially if students deem the role unpopular (like "Reporter"), use *Select and Switch*. In this strategy, the student who is selected for a role gets to choose someone else ... if she so desires!

Grouping Students

It's possible this strategy could fill an entire chapter. There are *many* ways to form random groups of students:

- *Traditional playing cards.* Have students draw cards and group them according to suits, face value, etc.

- *Toys.* For more fun and to keep within a reasonable budget, find low- or no-cost toys. Dollar stores are filled with all sorts of choices, such as packages of dinosaurs, frogs, insects, or small cars. You can have students draw from a bucket to form groups (e.g., all the four-legged animals get together, all the two-legged animals get together). You can also regroup students without having them draw additional toys (e.g., all the mammals get together, all the reptiles get together). Students can keep the toys or the teacher can reuse them. Over the years, the authors have used a variety of animals, plastic flowers, pipe cleaners, buttons, colored shapes, and stickers.

- *Famous couples.* Distribute small slips of papers to students, each with the name of half of a famous couple (Martha and George, in a history class, for example). This can be extended to famous trios (sine, cosine, tangent, in math) or famous quads (John, Paul, George, and Ringo, for fun in *any* class). Students have to get up out of their seats to find the classmates that complete their group.

- *Synonyms or parts of speech.* The teacher creates and distributes cards that have, for example, synonyms. All the students with words that mean the same get together as a group. Another choice is to have students group as "verbs," "nouns," and "adjectives."

Hi, Mac

Hi, Mac is a quick and fun way for students to find a partner with whom to work. Ask them to find a "Highly Intelligent Motivated Attentive (Able, Adaptable, Amiable) Classmate." They greet each other with "Hi, Mac!" and get organized so that they can work together on the next task.

Humdinger

This strategy is sure to bring many smiles and much laughter to the classroom. It is an ideal way to randomly place students into groups. Prepare slips of paper with the names of songs on them. Use songs that are current and known to your students, as well as songs like "Happy Birthday," "Jingle Bells," and "Twinkle, Twinkle, Little Star." Each student gets one slip of paper with a song title. It's important that they keep it a secret.

On the signal, everyone stands up and moves around the room *humming* their song. The task is to find the other students who are humming the same song. Set this up so that the number of slips for each song corresponds to the size you want each group to be. Once all the hummers are grouped together, they head to their seats and get ready to proceed with the lesson.

I Have, Who Has?

I Have, Who Has? is a class-builder that's loads of fun and gets students working with content *and* focusing on the important skill of listening. This activity will work with any content area.

The teacher prepares enough small cards (cut 3 × 5 index cards in half), so there is at least one for each student. If the number of cards exceeds the class size, give a second card to those students who are capable of paying attention to two cards at once. Each card has two separate lines: "I have …" on the top and "Who has …?" underneath. The cards are prepared so the question asked ("Who has …?") is answered on *only one* of the other cards (see the math examples on page 65). The teacher marks the card that begins the game with an * or other icon. The student with that card begins by reading out loud to the class "I have 4. Who has my number increased by 7?"

The student whose card answers the previous card's question reads her card: "I have 11." She then reads the question "Who has my number tripled?" Continue in this pattern until the final "Who has …?" leads back to the "I have 4" on the first card.

Next step? Shuffle and redistribute the cards. As a competition, the class could try to beat its previous time. When this strategy is employed, students are sure to *beg* for review time!

*I have 49. Who has the smallest 2-digit odd number?	I have 11. Who has the number of sides on a pentagon?
I have 5. Who has an even 3-digit number?	I have 248. Who has 7 less than me?
I have 241. Who has a number with a 3 in the ones place?	I have 643. Who has the only integer that is neither positive nor negative?
I have 0. Who has the largest 4-digit whole number?	I have 9999. Who has the product of 7 and 3?
I have 21. Who has my largest prime factor?	I have 7. Who has a number that could be the number of degrees in an obtuse angle?
I have 95. Who has 50 less than me?	I have 45. Who has an 8 in the tens place?
I have 587. Who has the number of degrees in a right angle?	I have 90. Who has me decreased by 30?
I have 60. Who has the mean of 5, 2, 6 and 3?	I have 4. Who has 7 squared?

Jigsaw

The *Jigsaw* strategy was first developed in the early 1970s by Elliot Aronson and his students at the University of Texas and the University of California. While not LOL funny, this strategy is very captivating and allows multiple opportunities for students to engage in conversation with their classmates, something they will surely relish. *Jigsaw*'s other strength is that it allows students to learn of a lot of content while individually only having to focus on one, small part. This develops teamwork and cooperation as each student will have to learn the other content pieces from classmates.

Let's use an example in which the teacher uses a newspaper article that describes a new scientific discovery. The teacher divides the article into four pieces of equal length and difficulty and labels them A, B, C, and D, respectively. Enough copies should be made so that each student gets one of the four pieces. For example, in a class of 25 students, the teacher should prepare six copies of pieces A, B, and C, and seven copies of piece D. After distributing the pieces, the teacher instructs students to silently read, jotting down any thoughts, notes, ideas, and questions as they go.

After they are done reading, students with the same piece join together and engage in conversation on their passages. Group members work together so that they become experts on their material. The students clarify within their group any questions that arise and become confident in their understanding of the material. The teacher may choose to offer specific prompts to guide the students through their work.

At a signal, the teacher asks the students to form heterogeneous groups, so each group has at least one student who has become an expert on each piece of the article. In a class of 25 students, there will be five groups of four students (A, B, C, and D represented) and one group of five. In the sixth group there will be an expert on A, B, C and two experts on passage D. Now, it's round-robin time as each student shares his or her piece with teammates, offering clarification when needed and responding to any questions. The teacher moves from group to group, monitoring the conversations. There are many different ways of adapting *Jigsaw* to the classroom situation: size of the groups, range of topics, length of time for groups to work together, and so on. The method of how students share can be specified for the entire class, for individual groups, or by letting each student choose.

Key Punch

As a team-building strategy, *Key Punch* has as its focus a number of 21st-century skills: collaboration, problem solving, creativity, and communication. This strategy is also used successfully in the business world.

Set up an area on the floor that measures about eight feet by eight feet. This space is called the "restricted area." Within the space, lay down thirty 8½ × 11 sheets of paper numbered from 1 to 30, arranged in five rows of six sheets each with the numbers jumbled up. Offer a scenario like this:

One of our school's computers, solely dedicated to scheduling extra days off for students *only*, has crashed. This class has been chosen to repair it. To fix the computer, one student at a time must enter the "restricted area," press the keys on the "keyboard" by touching them in *sequential order* from 1 to 30, and complete this task in less than thirty seconds.

There are three stipulations:

1. All team members must participate.
2. Only *one* person can be in the "restricted area" and touch the keyboard at any one time. If two or more team members contact the keyboard at once, the team must start again, beginning at 1, while the clock continues to advance. Although only one person is in the "restricted area," remaining team members are around the perimeter giving encouragement, rethinking the strategy and getting ready to make any necessary improvements.
3. Keys *must* be touched in sequential order. If any keys are touched out of order, the team starts over while the clock continues to advance.

Form teams and then select a team at random to go first. On the signal the clock starts and off they go! The team is not given any time to plan.

It is highly likely that this team will be unsuccessful (the authors have never seen the task completed correctly on a first try). Debrief the process as an entire class. Allow the next team sixty seconds to collaborate and then start the clock. At the end of sixty seconds, debrief again and continue the attempts as long as desired or until one team is able to "fix" the computer in the allotted time. Reflect on the entire process, allowing team members to share their thinking, planning, strategies, failures, and successes. Ask students to determine the application or lessons they learned from *Key Punch* that might be beneficial to their learning.

Learning Partners

As a way for students to work with different classmates on a recurring basis, this strategy is perfect. Teachers create a handout with three or four different icons. The icons can be purely for fun or content-related. For example, a social studies teacher might choose the three branches of government: executive, legislative, and judicial. Each student gets a copy of the handout with the three icons. The students' task is to find a different person to be their partner for each icon.

For example, two students, Keith and Eric, meet each other. Keith says to Eric, "Will you please be my judicial partner?" Eric agrees and writes "Keith" in his "judicial" space as Keith writes "Eric" in his "judicial" space. They are now judicial partners. They go their separate ways to partner up with two more classmates for their executive and legislative partners. Any students who cannot find a partner should raise their hand and a classmate or the teacher can offer assistance.

During instruction, when the teacher wishes to have students work with a partner, he asks students to look at their *Learning Partner* handout and find the partner associated with the icon the teacher names ("Get together with your judicial partner for the next task").

As with any strategy that asks students to independently find a partner, there may be those who will find this a little challenging. Some students are introverted, new to the school, or not well-liked by all classmates. When this happens, the teacher can intervene and ask another student if he or she would be willing to partner with the child in question. This gets the process started and can boost the confidence of the student who initially might have not been able to find partners on his or her own.

In order to use this strategy, the teacher must note any students absent on the day the handouts are first distributed. The teacher can fill in the names of classmates on the absent student's *Learning Partners* handout. Be sure to let the students whose names were selected know so that they can fill in the absent student's name on their own handout in the appropriate space.

In order for students to experience working with a variety of partners, teachers should consider repeating *Learning Partners* with different prompts on a regular basis.

MI Challenge

Even Gardner's (1983) multiple intelligences can find their way into a seriously fun classroom. The teacher chooses a number of topics that the class has been exploring and forms teams of students. For example, in an elementary art classroom, the topic could be the color wheel. Each team is assigned *one* of the types of colors found in the color wheel—primary, secondary, tertiary. It is perfectly acceptable for more than one team to share the same topic. Each team's task is to prepare a presentation on that topic for the class, using as many of the eight intelligences as possible. In order to promote a variety of intelligences, all presentations will be *Interpersonal*; *everyone* in the group will be involved. Groups are to use one or both of the "School Smarts": *Verbal/Linguistic* and *Logical/Mathematical*. Finally, students choose at least one of the remaining intelligences: *Visual/Spatial, Bodily/Kinesthetic, Musical/Rhythmic, Naturalist,* and *Intrapersonal*.

Set a time for preparation of about fifteen minutes. This time frame is appropriate in that it allows enough time for thinking, planning, and consensus yet not too long so that the teams lose their focus. Decide which team would like to go first. Each team presents to the entire class. Ask each member of the audience to make a note of *one* important content-related idea and identify which intelligences have been used. Feel free to use the following rubric as a means of assessment. Record the performances so you have an archive to be used as models for other students in the future and to provide fun and laughter for years to come!

	Beginning	**Developing**	**Competent**	**Accomplished**
Evidence of multiple intelligences	Presentation does not include all members or only uses "Interpersonal"	Presentation contains "Interpersonal" and "Verbal/Linguistic" or "Logical/Mathematical"	Presentation contains "Interpersonal" and "Verbal/Linguistic" or "Logical/Mathematical" and one other intelligence	Presentation contains "Interpersonal" and "Verbal/Linguistic" or "Logical/Mathematical" and at least two other intelligences

Continued

	Beginning	Developing	Competent	Accomplished
Content	Content in presentation does not demonstrate clear under-standing and has many errors	Content in presentation is fairly accurate with limited errors and misunder-standings	Content in presentation is accurate	Content in presentation is accurate and sup-ported with appropriate examples
Presentation	Presentation does not con-vey concept clearly to audience	Presentation conveys concept with minimal errors	Presentation is engag-ing and adequately conveys key concepts to audience	Wow! Wor-thy of Oscar nomination

Puzzling Connections

Most of us enjoy puzzles, and educators can capitalize on enjoyment by using illustrations related to content being studied. Comics, pho-tos, drawings, maps, and other content-related graphics are appro-priate choices. Print multiple copies of the selection on card stock and cut them into pieces, creating the parts of a puzzle. Create enough puzzles so that each student gets at least one piece of the puzzle. When the time arrives for students to form groups, they get together with the other two, three, or four classmates who have the pieces to complete the puzzle. Group members can then engage in conversa-tion about whatever the completed document represents.

Teammates Consult

Kagan Publishing and Professional Development created *Teammates Consult*, which focuses on the important 21st-century skill of col-laboration. The teacher prepares a set of content-related prompts that are given to students. Groups of three or four students place a cup within reach of each team member. Students put their writing utensils in the cup.

One student begins. She reads the first prompt, as the others *listen only*. Taking turns, all students, including the one who read the prompt initially, share their ideas, ask questions for clarification, and engage in general conversation. The objective is to come to consensus and prepare a response to the prompt.

Once the group has reached agreement, all students remove their pens from the cup and record the answer to the prompt on their paper. The teacher can choose either to have students prepare the exact same answer or have them put ideas in their words. The pens are returned to the cup and the process continues for each of the remaining prompts.

Uncommon Commonalities

As a team-builder, this strategy will have students working *very* hard. Arrange students in groups of three to five each. Their task? Discover as many commonalities among themselves as they can in a limited time period, usually two to three minutes.

Groups score one to three points for each commonality; the more unique, the more points. The teacher is the judge and awards points as she sees fit. For example, in a sixth-grade class, award one point for responses along the lines of "Each person is in sixth grade" or "Each person has a sibling." Two points are given for responses like "Each person was born in an odd-numbered month." A three-point response might be "Each person has an aunt born outside of this state." This strategy can go a long way in helping students understand more about each other while learning to work hard together to achieve a goal. The bonus is that they have fun.

This strategy also works for adult groups. Faculty members gathered for their monthly meeting, for example, might have the following responses: "The workday for each of us begins at 7:25" (1 point), "We all travel more than ten miles to get to work" (2 points), and "We all belonged to a Greek organization that shared a Greek letter" (3 points). Since the focus is on team-building, this is more of a sharing than a competition, although one never knows.

The Wizard

Standing in front of the class and giving a report has been a part of schooling for eons. *The Wizard* (Loomans and Kolberg, 2002) certainly puts a twist on that age-old practice.

Place students into groups of four or five. The SFR (Serious Fun Rating) can be raised dramatically by providing the group with a wizard's cape to wear. A large bedsheet draped over everyone's shoulders gives the illusion of a multiheaded wizard. A prompt or question is posed to the group. An example from a music class might be "What composer has had the biggest impact on music in the 21st-century classroom and why?" The teacher commands the Wizard to speak using one mind, although with many mouths. The response is given one word at a time. A group of four students might respond like this: Student 1: "Aaron"; Student 2: "Copeland"; Student 3: "had"; Student 4: "the"; Student 1 again: "biggest"; Student 2 again: "impact"; Student 3 again: "because" and Student 4 again: "he" (students continue in this pattern with "won … a … Pulitzer … Prize … for … music"). This example has each student replying multiple times. The teacher may require a minimum number of words in the answer to maintain academic rigor.

A wonderful adaptation would be to have two "Wizards" talking to each other about what they are learning in class. What fun!

Words Alive

Bringing words to life is important for anyone looking to be successful in the 21st-century. *Words Alive,* adapted from "Cloze to Close" by Bruce Wellman is a team-builder but also works very well as a piece of closure or review at the end of a unit of learning.

Individually, each student writes down one word that captures a salient point from the learning. Hyphenated and two-word phrases are acceptable. Form small groups of four students. The group's task then is to create one sensible and grammatically correct sentence using all of the words or phrases that were created individually.

Now, it's time to *really* bring those words to life. It is the group's choice of what to do next, such as creating a skit, poster, or song. Each group shares its finished product with the rest of the class.

Your Sentence Is Up

The objective of *Your Sentence Is Up* is for teams, without preparation time, to write sentences that summarize a piece of learning. Arrange the class into an appropriate number of teams. Having five or six members on each team will work well. Divide the whiteboard into the same number of sections as the number of teams. Line the teams up, front to back, single file, in front of their section of the whiteboard as far away as possible. There is one important caveat: team members are *not* allowed to communicate with one another.

On the signal, the first player in line "runs" to her group's section of the whiteboard and starts the sentence by writing *one* word. She "runs" back to the second person in line, handing off the marker, and takes her place in the back of the line. The second person goes to the board and writes a second word. The pattern continues in the same fashion with the understanding that the goal is to form a coherent sentence, one word at a time, that captures the learning objectives established by the teacher. Team members take turns going to the board as many times as necessary to complete their sentence. Meanwhile, the other teams are also creating *their* sentences on *their* sections of the board.

When the last team member has written the final word and the sentence is finished, the entire team sits down. Once all teams have finished, conversation about the content of the sentences can begin.

Chapter 7

Seriously Fun Strategies for Processing Content

*We do our children a disservice when we call learning
'work'. So much of what we learn takes place in play.*
—Robert Sylvester

When it's time for students to actually process and internalize new learning, teachers have a myriad of choices. For many years, the go-to choices were lectures, videos, reading from textbooks, and filling in worksheets. While there *is* a place for all those activities in the course of a lesson, this chapter includes strategies and activities designed to more actively engage learners in their "work."

Practice is crucial in order for students to learn content. And the more they practice (and practice correctly), the more likely they'll learn and remember. When practice has an element of fun, students will want to work more and harder … and learn.

Carousel

Carousel is a cooperative learning strategy that can be used before, during, and/or after any unit of study. Small-group and whole-class conversation, along with small-group and whole-class reflection, are major tenets of *Carousel*.

First, form small groups of three to five students. The teacher chooses a number of topics. For example, if a music class is studying genres, the teacher could choose rock, classical, alternative, and jazz.

Each topic is written as a heading on a separate piece of chart paper. The number of topics is equivalent to the number of groups. Groups stand in front of one piece of chart paper and are assigned a different colored marker specific to them.

Choose a designated length of time (one to two minutes works well) for group members to brainstorm and write as much information about their topic as they can on their piece of chart paper with their colored marker. When time expires, they leave their chart behind, grab their marker, and move clockwise to the next chart. The teacher resets the timer and starts it again. Once at the new chart, group members first read what the previous group wrote and engage in relevant conversation. Then, using their assigned marker color, they add to, embellish, comment, and write questions on the chart paper. Continue this process until each group is back at its original station.

Wrap up the activity by having a discussion about the topics on each piece of chart paper and reading and discussing what each group wrote, answering questions as necessary.

Final Word

Final Word is an excellent strategy that will work well with almost any piece of content: to prepare for a unit of study, review a homework assignment, after reading a piece of content-related material, or ending a unit. Arrange students into groups of three to five. The teacher poses a prompt, statement, or question to the groups.

Decide who goes first (see *For the Role of ...* in Chapter 6) and set a time limit of ten or fifteen seconds per person. The first person shares one point. Moving in a clockwise direction, each person in the group makes a comment or observation about what was initially shared, *without* interjection or comment from others in the group. The conversation comes back to the first person who then gets the final word. Consider allowing a little more time for this person to share.

The next person clockwise in the group takes the lead and the process is repeated. The strategy continues until each person has had a turn to get in the final word.

Four Corners

We all like to be able to make choices, and giving students the opportunity to choose is a good way to motivate them. Think about a unit of study. Select four different topics from the unit and write each at the top of a piece of chart paper. Post the papers in the four corners of the room. Students go to the corner of their choice and talk with others about the topic. Next, pair two students from different corners and have them share with each other their reasons for choosing that corner and what they discussed.

As a way to hold students accountable and get the entire class involved, conduct a class review. Pair students randomly and ask each member of the new partnership to speak about his or her corner's topic.

Graffiti Wall

Graffiti Wall begins with students placed into small groups. Each group receives one piece of blank 11 × 17 paper. Every person in the group gets a different colored marker. Decide which student will go first.

That student writes a word or short phrase that captures something he knows about the specific content being studied. The paper is passed to the next person, left or right. That person records a different note. Continue in this fashion until the paper returns to where it started. Repeat the process in the *opposite* direction for more words or phrases. Every word or phrase should be unique. Begin for a third and final pass. This time each student is to use a nonlinguistic representation.

Any student who cannot respond or add new information writes his name at the bottom of the paper. This allows the teacher to determine who might need additional support to master the content.

Hit the Target

When it's time to infuse some energy at review time, use this strategy. Cut a large variety of colored sheets of 8½ × 11 paper in half, horizontally ("hamburger" style). Give one piece of paper to each student. Ask students to record an important thought, idea, summarization, or question on their sheet of paper, along with their name. When everyone has finished writing, ask them to crumple their papers into a ball.

Next, designate the "target"—a bull's eye posted on the wall, a spot on the floor, a roped-off area in the room, a large basket or tub. On a signal, students throw their crumpled pieces of paper at the target.

All the students then pick up a piece that is a different color from the one they threw. They write on the back, reflecting and reacting to what their classmate wrote. Students might offer praise, contribute additional ideas, seek clarification, and so on. The uncrumpled sheets of paper can be returned to the original owner and/or collected for assessment purposes.

For a variation, have students crumple and toss the paper again to the designated target area after they have finished writing. Students choose again, a different color, and repeat the process as often as the teacher wishes.

Inside-Outside Circle

A fun, kinesthetic strategy, *Inside-Outside Circle* is a popular Kagan Publishing and Professional Development activity that gets students moving, talking, thinking, and listening ... and learning.

The teacher chooses a piece of content and a prompt. For example, for a middle school social studies class that is studying civil rights, the prompt might be "How did Martin Luther King's 'Letter from Birmingham Jail' support the use of civil disobedience to create awareness and change?"

Students count off, remembering their number. The "odds" form a circle, standing shoulder to shoulder with their backs to the center of the circle. They are Partner A. The "evens" form a similar circle facing a partner from the first circle. These students are Partner B. Partner A responds to the prompt first for about forty seconds. Then Partner B speaks for the same length of time, adding, embellishing, and/or paraphrasing.

Now it's time to move. All the A's move two (or any other number) people to the right (or left) to meet with a new partner. If desired, the same prompt can be repeated since there will be different pairs of students responding or the teacher can choose another prompt. Repeat the responding process described above but have partner B speak first this time. Time to move again. Repeat the prompt (or choose another), decide on how many spaces to move and in which direction. Students respond, A's first, then B's. Depending on the size of the class, teachers may have students move more or fewer times to complete the activity. This strategy can be another opportunity for formative assessment as the teacher stands in the center of the circle and listens to the conversations taking place.

Juggling Our Learning

After a specific period of study in class (twenty minutes, for example), ask all the students to think of something significant they learned in one or two words only. Next, form small circles of four or five students each. Toss a koosh ball to one person in each group. The person who catches the koosh states her significant learning to the others in the circle. She tosses the koosh to someone else in her small circle. He says, "Thanks. Your learning was _____ and mine is _____." He then tosses the koosh to a third person, who repeats the first two learnings, *in order*, and then adds his own. This continues for the entire circle until the ball gets back to the person who went first. With five students this sequence should take about a minute.

After a bit of a breather, start over again: same people, same order. Just for fun, have students share their responses a little faster than the first time. Continue this for as many rounds as desired, speeding things up a little more each time.

Paired Verbal Fluency (PVF)

PVF is a seriously fun strategy that focuses on listening. Students are paired. One is named Partner A and the other Partner B. For a little more fun, rather than "A" and "B," use two words related to the topic, like "single" and "cell" in science, or "musical" and "note" in music class. "Single" shares pertinent information on the topic for thirty seconds with "Cell," who *silently listens only*. When time is called, it's "Cell's" turn to speak for the same amount of time. However, "Cell's" information must be *new* information that was not mentioned previously. Next, "Single" shares only new information for twenty seconds while "Cell" listens. Again, switch roles. This pattern can be repeated as often as preferred and the times adapted to fit the teacher's needs.

Like many strategies, *PVF* can provide a chance for students to record their thinking and learning, reflecting on both the process and the content. As the class engages in *PVF*, the teacher moves around the room, listening to the exchanges and learning what the students know. The information gained by the teacher can be used as data for planning purposes.

Racking Up the Points

Getting ready for an upcoming assessment has never been more fun—or competitive! As a whole class, students individually and quietly study at their seats and review notes, text, or other sources of information for just two minutes. Once time is called, *all* materials are put out of sight.

Instruct students to record everything they can remember about the topic on a sheet of paper. Suggest that they might want to include all the big ideas from the unit and as many details as possible. Then form small groups and have students share their information with each other. Students individually add any ideas to their list that they didn't have when they created their own original lists.

Next, each student finds a partner from a different group. Students begin racking up points by earning one point for everything that they have on their list that is the *same* as their new partner. Students receive two points for each correct piece of information they have that their partner does *not* have. After one minute, partners tally their scores. They search for a different partner, compare lists again, and earn more points. Repeat this process as often as desired. After working with a predetermined number of partners, students return to their original groups.

Each group adds up the number of points won for each member on the team, calculating a group grand total. Class conversation can revolve around the items on everyone's list. This is an opportunity for the teacher to add any key points that may not have been mentioned by students.

Say Something

This strategy was created in order to give students a chance to read, think, talk, and listen (Short, Harste, & Burke, 1996).

Prepare passages for students to read. In a physical education class it might be a short article on the importance of aerobic activity. Give pairs of students two, three, or four paragraphs or passages on one sheet of paper. One passage will be used at a time. Each student independently and silently reads the first passage. When both have finished reading, each takes turns to "say something" to their partner about what they have just read. This conversation might involve summarizing the material, making a connection, offering a new idea,

• *Serious Fun* •

making a prediction, asking a question, and so on. If the teacher is so compelled, he can include a prepared prompt or two, asking students to respond.

After all the students have had a chance to say something, they return to their independent, silent reading of the *second* passage. The process repeats itself for all the passages. If desired, a formative assessment can be created by asking students to capture their thinking and learning after they have finished the entire article.

Chapter 8

Seriously Fun Strategies for Movement

Children at play are not playing about.
Their games should be seen as their most serious-
minded activity.

—Michel de Montaigne

Teachers have known for a long time that if students sit too long, trouble will ensue. That's why listening to lengthy lectures is not the best way for children to maximize learning. Periodically, the body and the brain need a break. Therefore, a teacher in a seriously fun classroom will have students out of their seats from time to time. The learning continues as students have a chance to get the wiggles out.

Research has found that content retention corresponds to motor development. In *Smart Moves: Why Learning Is Not All in Your Head* (1995), Dr. Carla Hannaford tells us that "physical movement ... plays an important role in the creation of nerve cell networks which are actually the essence of learning." When we are active physically, we are active mentally.

The cerebellum, the part of our brain that processes movement, is also a critical part of how we process learning. Multiple studies have demonstrated a strong connection between the cerebellum and cognitive functions like memory, spatial orientation, attention, language, and decision making. Movement expands blood vessels that allow for the delivery of brain food: oxygen, water, and glucose.

This research, of course, contradicts a long-standing, deep belief held by many educators that children learn best when they're sitting still, listening and working quietly at their desks, soaking up all the information sent their way.

So let's get students of *all* ages up and moving . . . and seriously learning!

Baggage Claim

In addition to providing students the chance to move, *Baggage Claim* can also be used as a class-builder or as a review activity. Distribute half-sheets of paper with an illustration of a piece of luggage or baggage icon. Students write their name on the luggage tag.

Students "pack their bags" by responding to prompts related to the content being studied. They write their responses directly on the piece of luggage. For example, for a third-grade class studying "fables, folktales and myths from diverse cultures" (CCSS: ELA. RL.3.2), three prompts might be the following:

1. What was the moral of the story?
2. How might *you* have handled the conflict in the story?
3. What is your dream vacation? (Note: it is important to include a fun prompt. This will allow an outlet for children to chat, which they'll do anyway, with or without their teacher's permission.)

Play an energizing piece of music for motivation and movement, like "On the Road Again" or "Leaving on a Jet Plane." Students gather up their bags and head off on their trip by moving around the room. When the music stops, the students freeze, partner with someone close by, and introduce themselves. They share the contents of their bag (their responses to the three prompts). At the end of the conversation (time limit of about a minute total), students trade bags with each other.

The music begins again and students move around the room. This time when the music stops, each student finds a *different* partner close by. For this round, students explain to each other that somehow they got the wrong piece of luggage. They take turns telling whose bag they have and what's in it. After about a minute, the music starts, the students trade bags *again* and continue in this fashion until time is up.

Once time has expired, students return to their seats. One at a time, they introduce to the entire class the person whose bag they are left with and share *one* of the responses "in the bag." After all have had the chance to share, the teacher facilitates class conversation about the prompts. By doing this, the teacher can adequately assess students' learning and knowledge. At a later, convenient time, each person returns the bag to its rightful owner.

Give One, Get One

This strategy is a version of one that comes from Kagan Publishing and Professional Development. Students can reflect on their learning by jotting down their thinking, moving around the room and engaging in conversation with their classmates. Students write down *one* thought or idea that captures their thinking about the lesson on a 3 × 5 index card. On the signal (for good movement music, see Appendix C), students begin to move around the room. They find a classmate and exchange their "ONE," verbally and physically (they swap cards). This pattern continues, giving a "ONE" and getting a "ONE" until the signal to stop is given. Once students have returned to their seats, they can take turns and share their observations about both the content and the process.

The Laugh-In Party

Given the popularity of syndicated television, some students might be familiar with the late 1960s television show *Laugh-In*. One segment of the show had cast members at "The Party," where music is playing and people are dancing. After a short while, the music stops. A camera zooms in and cast members give a ten-second monologue or dialogue. Then the music and dancing start again, and the process repeats.

The Laugh-In Party is based on "Mix-Freeze-Pairs-Discuss" from Kagan Publishing and Professional Development. The teacher chooses a number of prompts (the authors have found three to be perfect). Share the first prompt and have students start thinking about their response. Play an energizing piece of music. When the music starts, everyone mingles around the room.

When the music stops after twenty seconds, everyone freezes and quickly finds a partner nearby. Students spend about thirty seconds sharing their responses with each other. Once the music begins again, students thank their partners and continue mixing around the room. Repeat the process for the remaining question prompts, with students finding a *different partner* each time.

Students are offered the opportunity to stretch, move, think, talk, and reflect on their learning. Each of them gets to hear different thoughts and perspectives from their classmates as they all respond to the same prompt.

Line-Up/Wrap

This strategy is perfect for those lessons that call for students to voice a stance, share an opinion, or make a decision about how they feel about something being studied in class. And it gets them out of their seats for a little while. In a global studies class, students might be exploring the United Nations. Post the statement: "The UN is instrumental in solving problems throughout the world."

Students place themselves on a continuum from "Strongly Agree" to "Strongly Disagree" according to how they feel. They stand shoulder to shoulder, facing the same direction, forming a straight line. Next, "wrap" the line, with the far left person coming around to stand directly across from the person on the far right. This makes a one-to-one correspondence between students; if there is an odd number of students, the middle of the wrapped line will have a trio. The conversation that ensues is sure to be lively, even for those in the middle who will have similar thoughts and/or opinions.

A variation of *Line-Up* can be used to create groups. Arrange students sequentially based on a specific criterion, like their birthday (month and/or day) or the street number of their address; then the teacher can easily count students off into the desired group sizes.

Another variation is called *Circle the Wagons*. This is the same as *Line-Up* except that the students form a circle. Students count off, with the odd numbers pivoting counterclockwise on their left foot and the even numbers pivoting clockwise on their right foot so as to form pairs (or, if needed, one trio). This variation works better than *Line-Up* when space is somewhat limited.

Memory Mingle

When it's time once again for an energy break for the body *and* the brain, use *Memory Mingle* as a way for students' brains to make connections between words, words that on the surface might not seem to have any connection at all.

Students think of a key word or two-word phrase they associate with the lesson and record it on a 3 × 5 card. This word remains a secret … for now. Play a selection of music to get students up and moving. Have them mingle, saying hello to a classmate or two or three, all the while keeping their word a secret.

When the music stops, students quickly form trios. One at a time, they state their secret word. The trio then has to make *one* connection between those three words or phrases. On a fourth index card, the group writes the connection as a complete sentence with an explanation. The teacher collects the cards, shuffles them, and then selects a few for the entire class to discuss.

The Mixing Bowl

The Mixing Bowl is a strategy that has students moving, thinking, and interacting with many classmates. Students work cooperatively and expend a little energy. As with other strategies of this nature, the continual conversation and sharing allows teachers to observe and formatively assess student learning.

Students are placed into groups of four and then count off from 1 to 4. The teacher displays a content-related prompt. Each group has about a minute to work together and come up with a response to the prompt. All must be sure they understand the group's response.

After the minute is up, the teacher selects a number from 1 to 4 at random. The student in each group with that number stands up. As the teacher plays some energizing music, each student whose number was chosen moves to the next group in a clockwise direction. For example, if the teacher chose the number 2, all the 2s say goodbye to their first group and move clockwise to form a new group. Once the new group is settled, they engage in conversation about the prompt. The 2s bring their former group's perspective to the new group. Allow these newly formed groups a couple of minutes to talk.

When the new groups have finished, the teacher shares the second prompt. The new groups repeat the process of working together to form a response before a new number is drawn, at random, or the teacher chooses a number other than 2 to keep things mixed. The entire process repeats for as many prompts as the teacher has created.

Musical Bags

Musical Chairs is certainly a fun activity that can put anticipation, excitement, and a little movement into any room. *Musical Bags* takes that idea and confines it to a smaller space. Arrange students into small groups of four to six and seat them in a circle. Each group gets one paper bag containing slips of paper with prompts that relate to the learning. When the music starts, students begin passing the bag around their group. Just as in Musical Chairs, this continues until the music stops.

At that point, the person caught holding the bag removes one of the slips. He reads it out loud and then shares his response with the group. This slip can either stay out of the bag or be returned. The music starts again and the bag starts another journey around the group. Continue for as many rounds as desired.

Round the Room and Back Again (RTRABA)

An absolute favorite! Characteristics inherent in this strategy are academic rigor, movement, collaboration, memorization, assessment, and fun.

To begin, have students write down one piece of content-related information. Depending on when *RTRABA* is used, it could be something new to learn, something that was learned, or a key point. Encourage students to write the fact down and offer a sentence or two of clarification. After a couple of minutes, it's time for students to summarize their writing to the point where they can quickly and easily remember it and share it in just a few seconds.

On the signal ("I Get Around" by the Beach Boys is an excellent musical choice here), everyone places paper and writing utensils aside; they will not be needed for the next part of *Round the Room*. Students begin moving around the room, sharing their one piece of information and listening to and memorizing the ideas of their classmates. These conversations are very short, about fifteen seconds. These exchanges continue until the music stops (about two minutes). This time period is an adequate length of time for most students to fill up their brains.

Students return to their seats and individually write down all the thoughts and ideas they can recall. After a couple of minutes, create pairs or groups to combine individual lists. The teacher can choose to make this a competition to see which group can create the longest, unduplicated list.

RTRABA offers teachers fantastic formative assessment. Through observation, they can see what students remember or think is important in their learning.

Stand Up, Sit Down, Write, Write, Write

This is an ideal strategy to use just before an end-of-unit assessment (or *as* the assessment!). The teacher prepares three or four questions and/ or prompts. Begin by projecting the first prompt for all students to see. Students are given a few moments to think about what their response might be. Next, they place a blank sheet of paper at their desks.

The music starts and students stand up and begin moving around the room. When the music stops, they find a partner and engage in conversation about the first prompt. After about a minute, they sit down in nearby seats and write their responses on the paper at the seat.

When the music starts again, the students resume circulating around the room, leaving the papers at the seat. When the music stops, they quickly find a *different* partner. All eyes go to the front of the room for the second prompt. These two new partners share their thinking about that prompt. They then sit in a *different* seat and respond to the second prompt. Repeat until all the prompts have been addressed. When the final prompt has been shared, students return to their original seats to read and edit the responses their classmates left on the paper at their seat.

In *Stand Up, Sit Down, Write, Write, Write,* students get a review of content as well as the chance to listen to the differing perspectives of their classmates. If the teacher chooses to use *SUSDWWW* as an assessment, have students write their names on the top of the papers they originally left at their seats and turn them in to be reviewed.

Stepping Out of Line

Students should be offered frequent opportunities to express their opinions about what they are asked to learn. *Stepping Out of Line* allows students to express those opinions and enjoy the chance to get up out of their seats and talk with their classmates and teacher.

Provide a statement that requires students to take one of two sides (agree/disagree; support/oppose, etc.). For example, an earth science teacher might use the statement "Pluto should be reclassified as a planet." The students stand in a straight line, one behind the other. When given the signal, students take one step to the left if they agree with the statement or one step to the right if they disagree. If desired, pair up an agree with a disagree and have them engage in conversation. A prompt such as "What do you notice about where your classmates stood?" might be offered to stimulate their conversation.

Chapter 9

Seriously Fun Strategies for Closure

Learning is directly proportional to the amount of fun you have.

—Bob Pike

aster teachers know that the human brain can hold only so much information before deciding what to do with it (Jensen, 2005). After a while, the metaphorical cup starts to overflow. We can keep "pouring" more information into the brain, but most, if not all, of it will simply spill out and be of little use. The information just won't be retained. The importance of pausing periodically during instruction and asking students to summarize and review what they've learned cannot be overemphasized. Closure, as Madeline Hunter referred to it (Hunter, 1982), helps the brain move important knowledge into long-term memory. It is crucial that learners periodically summarize for themselves. Little, if any, learning moves to long-term memory when the *teacher* provides the summary of the learning. Providing ample time for closure can be one of the easiest, quickest, and most effective ways to improve learning in our schools.

Many teachers ask, "When or how do I find time for closure?" The answer is, "It depends." It's a teacher's decision as to when it's time to pause and let the brain process. There are no rules that say to stop after x minutes of instruction. However, here are three important points to remember:

1. A simple, rough estimate is to allow about one minute of information for each year of age of the students. For example, in an eighth-grade class, after twelve to fourteen minutes of new information, utilize one of the strategies in this chapter to allow students to process, organize, categorize, and retain the learning (Jensen, 2005).

2. Using the formula above, waiting until the end of a forty-five-minute class for closure is ill-advised. It is highly likely that new content will not make it into long-term memory.

3. Learning has a peak and flow. The human brain learns best at beginnings and ends of units of learning. Therefore, chunking the learning during class periods so that there are multiple beginnings and endings is advisable.

Some of the strategies in this chapter take less than sixty seconds to complete; others take longer. Some activities involve movement, and others have students working collaboratively. Also included are strategies that look a lot like "note-taking": fun and different ways for students to gather thoughts and ideas so that they remember what they are learning.

2-1 (3-2-1, 5-3-1, etc.)

There are many opportunities for students to read and react or respond to what they are learning. Setting aside class time to just read may seem to be an efficient use of time, but the reality is that, since there is no accountability, the page or paragraph may not be read or understood. Instead, consider assigning the reading and then asking the student to come up with two key points and one question to ponder. This is known as the *2-1* strategy.

When selecting a reading passage, the teacher should choose one at an appropriate reading level, of adequate length and, most importantly, one that presents academically rigorous information specifically targeting the desired learning objectives. The reading might be a newspaper article, a primary document, a crucial piece from a textbook, an outside reading that requires students to delve more deeply into the learning, or a summary of different perspectives. The reading could also be used as an anticipatory set to begin a conversation. The teacher gives students time to read and complete the *2-1* by recording two important learnings and one question they still have. In the next step, the teacher asks students to share one of their learnings or their question with a partner and then be ready to share with the whole group. When students are held accountable for their work—that is, when they understand they will be sharing their thinking with others—the likelihood of their completing the reading increases. There is an opportunity for students to interact with one another and for the teacher to monitor the conversations. The teacher is thus able to have his fingers on the pulse of the class. Do they all get it? Are some students struggling? Do *none* of the students get it? This moment provides a decision point for the teacher as he determines whether to move on, review, provide spot help, or engage in whole-group conversation. The teacher can vary the *2-1* prompts to suit the students and the material being read—for example, requiring three (or five) key words or phrases, two (or three) important points, and one take-away question.

Aha! Slips

Aha! Slips are small pieces of paper used by students to gather thoughts, ideas, and notes on the content being studied. As students discover an interesting idea, come across a very important point, see something that is a real keeper, or just have an "Aha!", they record it on one of the slips. The students collect the slips throughout the unit of study, referring to them as a means of review. For assessment purposes, the teacher might randomly call upon students to share one of their "Aha!"slips with others.

Bag of Tricks

Bag of Tricks is a great way to gather thoughts, ideas, and notes. Each student receives a plain, white, paper bag. Ask them to decorate the bag with crayons, markers, and/or colored pencils, including their name and the topic being studied. Make available a number of *Aha! Slips* for students to use. As they record their insights, they drop the slips into their *Bag of Tricks*.

At different times during the learning, the teacher can ask students to reach into their bag, remove a slip, and reflect. They can share with a partner, swap bags and have a classmate choose a slip at random, or choose one and write a possible test question with the information. The teacher could choose to collect slips from students to use as formative assessment, finding out what they know (or don't know) and what they are thinking. The possibilities are almost endless. Note-taking has never been more fun!

Beach Ball Review

Inflatable balls (beach or otherwise) come in different sizes and can be purchased from mail-order catalogues, websites, and discount stores. When it's time for an energizing strategy that formatively assesses student learning, get a beach ball ready to go. Arrange six or seven students into a circle. A typical class will need multiple beach balls, one per group. Start a piece of music; "Surfin' USA" by the Beach Boys works perfectly. Students gently toss the beach ball around their group. After fifteen seconds, stop the music. The student holding the beach ball shares a significant learning or any other prompt designated by the teacher. Continue for a few more rotations. This strategy can be used many times during the school year and never gets old.

Bright Idea

Bright Idea is an opportunity to offer students a fun, novel, and different way to record information. For *Bright Idea*, have available quarter sheets of paper with an illustration of a lightbulb. Encourage students to use these sheets any time they want to record important learning: a reflection in or out of class, a realization discovered when playing a game, or a summary statement after a reading, video, or lecture.

Perhaps the most fun that can be had with *Bright Idea* is to supply full-size sheets of paper with the illustration and ask students to do their homework on it. The authors have found that homework compliance increases dramatically; it's just more fun than the traditional piece of lined paper. For variety, use illustration items that are relevant to your students (i.e., T-shirt, sneaker, bicycle, car, guitar, football; the list is endless). The relevancy of icons such as these will increase the likelihood of students using these papers … and completing their work.

Exit Card/Ticket Out the Door

This well-known and time-tested strategy can hold students accountable for their learning as they leave the classroom and give teachers a perfect tool for assessment. Think of a prompt. You can start with the basic ones:

- What did you learn today?
- What was one key idea?
- With which learnings do you still need help?

Depending on the time available, you could also increase the fun factor a little with these suggestions:

- If you were to construct a building with important learnings from today, how many stories would it have? Explain.
- Write one verse of a song about today's lesson (it doesn't have to rhyme).
- If this lesson were the ingredients of a sandwich, what would you include?
- Write a news headline based on what you learned today.
- Turn today's important learnings into a meal. What would be your appetizer, entrée, and dessert?
- Write a "Teenie Tweet" (less than forty characters) of your learning today.
- Send a text message to a younger friend or family member. What would you say to make your friend understand what we did today?

It is entirely the teacher's professional decision as to what to do with these exit cards. They can provide excellent formative assessment.

Focused Reading

Many educators know that one of the worst things to say to students is simply "Read this material." If learning and remembering are important goals, then reading must have a focus or purpose. When assigning a reading passage, ask students to take notes following presented prompts. There are many ways to do this. A few suggestions are listed below:

- *2-1 (3-2-1, 5-3-1, etc.).*
- Mark an important point with a checkmark, new learning with an exclamation point, questions you have with a question mark.
- Note one thing you "knew," one thing that is "new."
- Note something you "know," something in which to "grow" (you want to learn more).
- Mark new learning with a plus sign, something you don't understand with a minus sign, an interesting fact you learned with a capital I.

Give Me Five

Give Me Five is a version of the strategy *Thumbs Up, Thumbs Down*. In *Give Me Five*, the teacher poses a prompt, usually asking how much of the topic the student understands. On the count of three, students hold up the appropriate number of fingers to represent their level of understanding of the content. So that there is a consistent representation for all, use the following signals:

- All five fingers—"I know it so well I could teach it."
- Four fingers (hold down thumb)—"I got it and know it pretty well."
- Three fingers (hold down thumb and index finger)—"I understand about half and don't understand the other half."
- Two fingers (hold down thumb, index finger, and middle finger)—"I only get some of it."
- Pinky only—"I understand very little (or maybe even none) of it."

Keeper/Leaper

After reading/listening/watching, pause and ask students to share one thing that for them is a real "keeper" and one thing that might require a stretch or "leap" to get it right.

Links to Learning

This strategy creates a three-dimensional visual in the classroom that reminds students what they are learning is important. The teacher cuts 8½ × 11 colored sheets of paper into eight equal strips. As a model, link a few strips into a chain using tape, paper fasteners, or staples. Keep a large number of blank strips in a location convenient for student access. During class, whenever students have new ideas, questions, or significant learnings, they get a strip and neatly write their thought on one side. At an appropriate time, they get up and add their strip to the chain.

After a set period of time (a class period or multiple class periods), students and/or the teacher can take the chain apart and distribute links to everyone. Reflection and conversation commence.

MIP/MVP

At the end of a piece of content, ask students to select an *MIP/MVP:* "Most Important Point/Most Valuable Point." They can record their *MIP/MVP* in their notes, silently reflect upon it, or discuss it with a partner.

Six-Word Memoirs/Six-Word Stories

Summarizing has met its match with *Six-Word Memoirs*. What if you were asked to write a memoir of your life … and could use only six words?! It is said that novelist Ernest Hemingway was once challenged to write a short story in only six words. Larry Smith and Tim Barko (en.wikipedia.org/wiki/Six-Word_memoirs) decided they wanted to do the same thing.

Start by using the original *Six-Word Memoirs* as they were created by Smith and Barko. Give students time to write a personal six-word summary of their lives. Their memoirs might be funny, inspirational, profound, mundane, or clever. These could be shared and displayed as a class-builder.

An academic variation of *Six-Word Memoirs* is *Six-Word Stories*. When it's appropriate during the course of study, students can summarize content knowledge in the same way. Here is a list of a few possible *Six-Word Stories*:

- Character education: *Good character includes respect and responsibility.*
- Health: *Bicycle safety requires a proper helmet.*
- Chemistry: *Ions: atoms with charged valence electrons.*
- And from the authors: *Learning is serious business ... and fun!*

Teenie Tweet

Twitter©, the popular 21st-century social medium, can have a place in the classroom, using 20th-century (and earlier) technology. One of the strengths of Twitter© is that it asks users to summarize and compose messages of 140 characters or less. A *Teenie Tweet* is a tweet of a Twitter© tweet. When time is short (or the teacher wants students to be even more concise), have them use forty characters or less to summarize their thoughts and learnings. This is a perfect strategy to use in the classroom, and students will undoubtedly love it.

Think-Pair-Share (TPS)

Without a doubt, *Think-Pair-Share*, created by Frank Lyman (1981), is familiar to many a teacher. Students are presented with a prompt about the content they are currently exploring. They use individual think time to formulate a response. After a short while, students pair up with a classmate and share their thinking.

To take *TPS* to the next level, make it *TPSS* by adding "Square." Place two pairs together and have the foursome engage in conversation. As an assessment tool, students can be asked to record their thinking and share it with the teacher.

Twenty-Second Speech

A number of different skills can be practiced with this strategy: reflecting, summarizing, organizing, and public speaking. Once a specified unit of learning has finished, pair up students. The goal is to prepare a speech that lasts twenty seconds, give or take a few seconds, summarizing a targeted piece of the learning. Both partners must speak. Using notes is allowed and encouraged.

As each speech is delivered, the rest of the class listens carefully, jotting down salient points from the speech in their notes.

One adaptation is to make the speech similar to a news or press conference. After the speakers have finished, they can take questions from the audience. Who knows—perhaps the next great public speaker will be discovered in your class!

Chapter 10

Seriously Fun Content-Specific Activities

By engaged learning, we mean that all student activities involve active, cognitive processes such as creating, problem-solving, reasoning, decision-making, and evaluation. In addition, students are intrinsically motivated to learn due to the meaningful nature of the learning environment and activities.

—Kearsley & Shneiderman

The previous chapters include strategies, activities, and ideas that cross discipline boundaries. They can be used with almost all students, regardless of grade level, content, or skill. This chapter will veer from that course and hone in on activities specific to a content area and grade level. These activities have been selected to represent a range of grade level and content areas. The charge for the professional is to examine, reflect upon, and make the necessary adaptations to these activities so that success (and fun) abound.

When you choose an activity to use in your classroom, make sure that it is a good fit for what you are trying to accomplish. There should be specific learning outcomes that are appropriate. You should not be using an activity just to do an activity. Also consider that, even if the learning outcome is well defined, spending hours and hours to prepare for an activity that is over in less than ten minutes may not be the best way to present the concept or the best use of your valuable time. There are times when direct instruction is best. As you plan lessons, ask these questions: "Does this strategy enhance my students' acquisition of the concept or skill in a timely manner?" and "Will my students be more engaged in their learning if I choose this activity?"

While paging through this chapter, you'll want to start with what's presented and then adapt or create your own activities to fit the learning and your own personal teaching style. Make use of these activities as a springboard to create your own and consider how to incorporate 21st-century skills in the design. Barney Dalgarno said, "Choose activities likely to facilitate the achievement of specific learning outcomes.... Learning occurs primarily through the learner's activity, rather than through passively receiving information" (Dalgarno, 1998). Does the activity provide opportunities for the students to collaborate? Having the opportunity to think out loud, explore resources with others, and discuss the different sides of a topic all lead to richer solutions. The ability to work with others on a team to reach a conclusion is something that is desired in higher education and the workforce. It is a 21st-century skill.

Novelty for the brain is like candy. Activities should hook students. This can be achieved by tapping into something that is out of the ordinary. The brain seeks out novelty and pays attention to it, allowing the learner to spend more time with the material. If the activity selected to introduce or reinforce specific content and/or skill lacks novelty, the brain is likely to drift to another place that is off topic. Continuous presentation of facts or repetition of skills does not prime the pump of a student's brain for learning.

Relevance is paramount to learning and retention. Structure the activity so that it contains something that the student might see or experience in real life. The closer the connection a classroom has to the real world, the more likely the student can transfer the content knowledge to novel situations.

Adopt or adapt these activities so that they meet with your objectives. You are sure to hook students and make them want to come back for more.

Out Into the Real World *(Business)*

Many community nonprofits need volunteers with business and marketing expertise, and our schools are ripe for the picking. Before the beginning of the semester, meet with local nonprofit groups and determine which groups would like assistance in getting their message out to the public.

Divide your students into groups of a manageable size. At the beginning of the semester, arrange for each student group to meet with a nonprofit representative to whom they have been assigned. At the initial meeting, the representative discusses the organization's mission, vision, and long-term goals with the students. Throughout the semester, as marketing and business strategies are introduced and explored, students apply their new learnings to the work of the nonprofit organization. The students and the nonprofits work closely together in real work that is relevant and has an impact beyond the classroom. Whenever students can be engaged and involved in work that is necessary and relevant, there is serious fun to be had.

Source: Nolte (2008)

Getting Out the Info
(English Language Arts: Literature)

Using whatever piece of literature students are reading, have them write a point-of-interest or informational brochure for the setting. Books with multiple settings provide choice for the students. For example, if the students are reading a Harry Potter novel, the brochure might highlight Diagon Alley, Hogwarts, Hogsmeade, or the Ministry of Magic. If students are reading a book as a class, like *The Adventures of Tom Sawyer*, they might create a brochure extolling the virtues of St. Petersburg, Missouri, in the mid-1800s. If studying *The Giver*, students can map out the region and the Community, pinpointing some of the significant buildings (House of Old, Department of Justice, the Nurturing Center, the Childcare Center, the Food Distribution Center, Auditorium, Hall of Open Records, the Annex). This activity allows students to display their knowledge of the setting and reinforces the use of technology as they create a professional-looking brochure that contains information about the book and the characters to share with peers.

Magnetic Word Poetry *(English Language Arts: Speech/Communication)*

Students begin by studying parts of speech. Once the teacher has assessed students and knows they have a clear understanding of the topic, they compile a list of 185 creative, descriptive words—50 verbs,

40 nouns, 20 adjectives, 20 adverbs, 15 conjunctions, 15 interjections, 10 pronouns, and 15 prepositions. The students can work individually, with a partner, in a small group, or as a whole class. The students keyboard the words, one to a line, double-spaced, in a standard bold font and size (Times New Roman 18 will work well). The document is printed and the words are cut into strips and placed on magnetic tape that is then cut to size. The students create poetry using their magnetic poetry pieces. They practice their poetry and then have a poetry slam. If desired, students can produce podcasts of the poetry selections to be posted on the class website.

Source: Faulkner (2012)

Tom Swifties *(English Language Arts: Writing and Composition)*

Tom Swifties are well known to many educators and can be an appropriate and engaging activity for students in the intermediate grades through high school. The instructor introduces Tom Swifties when the lesson objective is to help students think about how to enhance their word choice and add interest for the reader. Tom Swifties can also be used as an exercise to teach students how to accurately punctuate dialogue or to help them understand the use of puns in writing.

Work with your school librarian to get a few Tom Swift books to use. If an actual Tom Swift book cannot be secured, you can find online excerpts to read. Next, provide background for the Tom Swift series of books. The Stratemeyer Syndicate released the Tom Swift series under the pen name of Victor Appleton. The main character of the series is a young scientist, Tom Swift, who creates inventions that are well ahead of his time. When writing dialogue, the authors characteristically modified the phrase "he said/she said" with an adverb—for example, "'No professor?' cried Miss Perkman indignantly" and "'I—I don't know what to say,' stammered Tom" (Appleton, 1910).

From that, Tom Swifties evolved. In a typical Tom Swifty, the quoted sentence comes first, followed by the description of the act of speaking, using an *-ly* adverb, a verb pun, or a pun phrase.

- *-ly* adverbs
  - "If you want to play a long shot, Las Vegas has the underdog at 20 to 1," said Tom oddly.
  - "We're all set to visit Antarctica," Tom said icily.

- verb puns
  - "There's room for one more," Tom admitted.
  - Tom spoke: "I was going so fast over that bump, the wheel on my bicycle broke!"
- pun phrases
  - "I love hot dogs," said Tom with relish.
  - "I won't finish in fifth place," Tom held forth.

Have individuals brainstorm synonyms for "said." Once they have a lengthy list, take them through an example. For example, one could write, "'The sun is rising,' Tom said" or one could use a Tom Swifty and write "'The sun is rising,' Tom mourned."

Once students understand the task, set them loose to create their own Tom Swifties. Reserve class time for individuals and groups to share their best ones.

Source: Harrison (n.d.)

Real-Life Fair: Career Exploration and Household Budgeting
(Family and Consumer Science)

This activity is larger in scope than many of the activities outlined in this book but may be worthwhile to consider when planning a career unit. It was first executed in Exeter-West Greenwich (Rhode Island) Junior High School, where middle school students in the Family and Consumer Science class completed a survey about their aptitudes, likes, and dislikes and then explored careers that corresponded with their survey results. Teens receive instruction in how to use the Bureau of Labor Statistics (BLS) Career Information and *Occupational Outlook Handbook* (http://www.bls.gov/ooh). Using these resources, students determine the gross starting salary and the educational requirements for the profession that they chose. As a part of the unit, the net salary is calculated using a current national average rate, and from that figure, students determine the monthly take-home pay.

The budgeting begins! To start, students put aside 10 percent of their take-home pay for a personal savings program. The teacher secures sample checkbook ledgers and blank checks from a community bank or credit union. A representative from one of these local institutions might speak to the students about how to budget and use a checkbook properly. Students record their net salary after savings in the ledger. The students brainstorm the typical needs of an adult—housing (generally 20 percent of the balance), transportation (15 percent of the balance), food, clothing, insurance, real estate taxes and recreational possibilities.

Once each student's take-home pay and budget are set, a *Real-Life Fair* is planned. Booths with displays and information about each of the budgeted areas are set up and manned with community business representatives. Here are some examples:

- Housing: at this booth, students choose a mortgage or rental based on 20 percent of their monthly salary.
- Transportation: students use advertisements to choose transportation based on 15 percent of salary.
- Insurance: based on housing choice, students purchase homeowners' or rental insurance and automobile insurance.
- Financial advice: students invest 10 percent of their original net income in stocks, bonds, annuities, and other products with a financial adviser.
- Food and clothing: students spend $125 on food and $50 on clothing at this booth.
- Student loans: if postsecondary education is required for their job, they set up a monthly loan payback system.
- Part-time jobs: if a student wishes to supplement his income, he may choose from a list of real part-time jobs posted.
- Recreation: based on remaining income, students subscribe to phone, Internet, cable TV; get a gym membership; go on a vacation, etc.

At a minimum, booths with community business representatives should be created for housing, transportation, insurance, food, student loans, investments, part-time jobs, and recreation (Internet, cable, travel, restaurants). Each booth is stocked with a number of calculators. Students rotate through the booths. At each booth, the students review their budget and work with a representative to determine what they can afford. The student writes a check for the monthly expense and deducts the amount from the ledger. The representative takes the check and initials or stamps the ledger entry before the student moves on to the next booth. In addition to the aforementioned booths, there is an information booth to provide assistance to students who are struggling with the task. The next-to-the-last stop is a ledger station where volunteers review students' ledgers for accuracy. The final stop is the Life Event Booth, where students randomly draw a card designating various unforeseen events (much like Monopoly's Chance and Community Chest cards). These cards might be labeled "Traffic Accident: $800 to repair car," "Work Bonus: $500," "Found $20 on sidewalk," and so on.

At the conclusion of the fair, students reflect on their job choice and what that will mean for them in "real life." This conversation often will lead to the establishment of new short- and long-term goals. At each point along the way, there are opportunities for conversation about careers, budgeting, community resources, and goal-setting. And it is almost guaranteed that some students will say, "This was fun!"

Source: Bafile (2000)

I **Am** ? *(Health)*

This is a game that can be applied to any unit of study in health (and other subject areas). Ideally it should occur at the end of a unit of learning. *I Am?* encourages students to be well organized and able to access information so that they can pose good questions and correctly respond.

At the end of the unit, the teacher prepares multiple sets of "I Am" statements that summarize the learning from the unit of study. For example, after the class has studied the importance of vitamins and minerals, slips might read *I am vitamin A, I am calcium, I am vitamin E*, etc. Students are grouped into trios. Each trio gets a container with five *I Am* slips. One student (Student A) in each trio is selected to be the leader and randomly pulls an *I Am* strip. Student B asks a question of Student A aimed at determining what is on the slip; the question should have a yes or no response. Student A responds. If Student B wishes to guess what the *I Am* is he may, but if the guess is incorrect, he loses a turn and Student C now can ask *two* consecutive questions. If Student B does not choose to guess, play passes to Student C, who asks one question of Student A. This continues until one of the students guesses correctly the *I Am*. That person then assumes the role of the leader and draws the next *I Am* slip, and the game continues with the new players. Once the instructions for the game have been given and the game starts, the teacher can move about the classroom monitoring the types of questions posed and the responses, clearing up misunderstandings.

Here's one example: Player A pulls a slip that reads *I am Vitamin A* and keeps it hidden. Player B asks the first question: "Can you be found in orange juice?" Player A responds, "No." Player B doesn't choose to guess and play passes to Student C. She asks, "Are you water soluble?" Player A says, "No." Player C doesn't choose to guess and play passes back to Player B, who asks, "Are you fat soluble?" "Yes" is the reply. Player B says that he wants to guess and says, "I am Vitamin E." This is incorrect. Play now goes to Player C, who can ask two questions. If she does not choose to guess at the end of her two questions, play passes back to Player B and the game continues in this fashion until someone correctly guesses the *I Am*.

Students can access notes or other reference materials to help them formulate and answer the questions posed. The teacher should leave a small block of time at the end of *I Am* to debrief and review any questions that arose.

Personal Dictionaries
(Information Literacy)

After the class reads *Freak the Mighty* by Rodman Philbrick (1993), take time to review and discuss the entries in the dictionary in the back of the book. Discuss with students the process for including words in dictionaries. Work with students and research the New Oxford Dictionary entries. Questions to ask: What do you think might be a word included next year? What is the format of entries in dictionaries? Present the task, which requires students to create a personal dictionary of words they use frequently, similar to the one Freak made.

In the back of *Freak the Mighty* is Freak's Dictionary. Included are words that Freak used in his everyday vocabulary, most of which have an unusual meaning in Freak's eyes. For example, Freak uses the word "ornithopter" and defines it as "a big word for a mechanical bird" (p. 166). Students may also add to their dictionaries words whose definitions are simply a creation of their imagination. For example, Freak includes the word "unicorn" and defines it as "a horse who makes a point" (p. 168). Students must include at least twenty words in their dictionary. The entries should be presented in the format of a formal dictionary entry. A sample rubric is included on page 109.

	Beginning	**Developing**	**Accomplished**	**Exemplary**
Personal dictionary has a minimum of 20 words	0 to 8 words included in personal dictionary	9 to 19 words included in personal dictionary	20 words included in personal dictionary	More than 20 words included in personal dictionary
Content	Few words are clearly defined Graphics and illustrations do not clearly connect with the words being defined	Some words are clearly defined Some graphics and illustrations are included	Most or all words are clearly defined Appropriate graphics and illustrations are included	Words are clearly defined Images and graphics that accompany the definitions help the reader to thoroughly understand the definition
Presentation	Viewer is distracted by the organization Cover lacks appeal for the reader	Font size may not be appropriate Background, visuals, and/or graphics are distracting Cover is somewhat appealing for the reader	Good use of color, font size, graphics, and information Cover is appealing and appropriate for a dictionary	Exemplary use of color, font size, graphics, and information Cover is appropriate for a dictionary and draws the reader's attention
Mechanics	Many spelling, capitalization, and grammar errors Few entries follow the appropriate format for inclusion in a dictionary: word entry, pronunciation, part of speech, definition, synonyms, word origin	Some spelling, capitalization, and grammar errors Some entries follow the appropriate format for inclusion in a dictionary: word entry, pronunciation, part of speech, definition, synonyms, word origin	Few spelling, capitalization, and grammar errors Most entries follow the appropriate format for inclusion in a dictionary: word entry, pronunciation, part of speech, definition, synonyms, word origin	Spelling, capitalization, and grammar are error-free All entries follow the appropriate format for inclusion in a dictionary: word entry, pronunciation, part of speech, definition, synonyms, word origin

I'm Away on a Business Trip
(Foreign Language)

Students are given the role of manager of a company that is hoping to expand business into a country that speaks a language other than English. For example, in a Spanish class, the company is looking to relocate to Mexico. The students' task is to prepare the sales force for a trip to Mexico that will take place in one week. The sales force will have an interpreter traveling with it. The trip itinerary will dictate what Mexican cultural elements need to be introduced to the sales force. After identifying and anticipating the specific aspects of Mexican culture that the sales force needs to become familiar with, the managers (students) need to prepare training with a timetable for the instructor. Students will present the plan to their supervisor (teachers and classmates) for review.

Here is one possible trip itinerary:

1. Fly into Mexico City Sunday afternoon
2. Formal dinner Sunday night with prospective clients
3. Monday morning breakfast at hotel
4. Midmorning tour of prospective client's facilities and a tour of the city
5. Informal lunch with prospective clients
6. Team sales presentations
7. Art exhibit showcasing Diego Rivera at the Frida Kahlo Museum
8. Casual dinner with sales colleagues prior to flight home.

Because your sales force members have no experience with Mexican culture, you must prepare them before they leave on the trip. After identifying specific aspects of culture in which your sales team needs to be trained (etiquette, dining, art, industry, highlights of major cities), prepare your training. It may take the form of factsheets, video, Internet clips, and/or presentations, along with a training schedule. Students are to be reminded that they only have one week to prepare the sales force.

Source: S.O.S. for Information Literacy (n.d.)

Math Munchers
(Mathematics: Algebra)

Math Munchers is a great (and very fun) way to help students foster teamwork through development of a team strategy. Team-building is modeled for students as the math and physical education teachers work together. For this strategy, the bigger the space (think gymnasium), the better. The game is based loosely on Pac-Man, a video game from the early 1980s. The winner is the first team to create and solve an equation (CCSS: Math.4.OA). The instructor takes thirty to fifty ping-pong balls and, using a permanent marker, labels them with variables, numerals, and other appropriate mathematical symbols. The teacher divides the class into groups of five students. Each team clusters around its home base, which is designated by a hula hoop.

Each team's home base is equidistant from the center of the playing area. Cones are placed in the center of the area, one for each team. Under each cone is an equal number of ping-pong balls labeled with numbers and mathematical symbols. Before beginning, the teacher tells the students how many symbols or numbers are to be used for the equation. On the teacher's signal, each team sends one player to the center playing area to retrieve a ball from under the cone. That player runs with the ball to the base, places it in the hoop and tags the next runner on the team. The tagged team member runs to the *same* cone and retrieves the next ball. While the teams' runners are accumulating ping-pong balls from the team's cone, the remaining team members are working together to create an equation. This continues until the team has the number of balls equal to the number of balls designated to create the equation. For example, if the teacher stated that there would be six numbers and/or symbols in the equation, each team would have six ping-pong balls in its hula hoop.

Once a team has the correct number of balls, members may choose to exchange their numbers or symbols for numbers and symbols under a *different* team's cone. Each player must place his or her ball in the home base (hula hoop) and tag the next runner before the student can exchange for another ball. The process continues until a team wins by creating an equation with the designated number of balls. As soon as an equation has been created, team members yell "Solved!" The other teams review the equation to be sure that it is correct. If it is, that team is declared the winner of the round, the balls are returned to the cones, and the next round begins. To give the students more ownership, have *them* create the symbols and balls for the next time the game is played.

Some important guidelines:

1. Players may never have more numbers and symbols at their base than the number of balls designated for the equation.
2. Players can retrieve only one ball at a time.
3. Players can remove balls from either their own cone or the cone of one other team *after* they have the designated number of ping-pong balls in their home base. They must return one ball at the same time so as to keep at the designated number.
4. Players must take the number or symbol that they uncovered. They cannot exchange in the center playing field without first taking the ball back to home base.

Variation: As with any game, ratchet up the rigor. For example, in the next round, the team that wins is the team whose solution has the highest value.

Source: Gates (n.d.)

"Vi"ing for Attention and Learning
(Mathematics: Geometry)

Using technology to engage students in their learning is an extremely effective way to hook students. There are a number of videos on the Internet that you can access to teach key concepts. Some are very, very good; others are frighteningly bad. It is important that you review the video in its entirety before using it to be sure that it is appropriate. Here are two questions to ask:

- Does this video match my learning objective?
- Does this video adhere to the behavioral standards of my school?

Vi Hart creates mathematics videos on a wide variety of secondary mathematical topics. She calls herself a "recreational math-emusician" and her work aligns perfectly with the idea of serious fun. As a young student, Ms. Hart was often not engaged in her schoolwork. At the age of thirteen, she attended a computational geometry conference with her father: "It was so different from school, where you are surrounded by this drudgery and no one is excited about it. Any gathering of passionate people is fun ... no matter what they're doing" (Chang, 2011).

Vi Hart graduated from college with a music degree but was unable to find work in her field. She began to take the doodles from the margins of her college mathematics notebooks and create videos using the content. The videos are very fast-paced, novel, and narrated by Vi herself. Some of her most watched videos are those explaining hexaflexagons. And in case you think that Ms. Hart's videos can only be appreciated by high-school students, watch this video of a student who is a bit younger and *totally* engaged in creating hexaflexagons: http://ronypony.blogspot.ca/2012/09/hands-on-explorations-math-geometry.html. Here is the link for Ms. Hart's videos: http://www.youtube.com/watch?v=VIVIegSt81k&feature=watch_response_rev.

There are many other videos that are relevant, amusing, engaging, and right on target for different learning objectives. As you study different topics, ask students to find videos and bring them to your attention so that you can share with other students. Better yet, have your students create their own videos and post to YouTube or TeacherTube.

Roller Derby *(Mathematics: Probability and Statistics)*

The number of fun ways to incorporate number cubes (dice) into the mathematics classroom is almost endless. The dice game *Roller Derby* is a favorite. The object is to place markers on a numbered game board and remove them as quickly as possible using the fewest number of rolls. The first time the game is introduced, students play individually at their seats using the teacher's rolls.

Each student has a simple game board and twelve markers, such as buttons or beans.

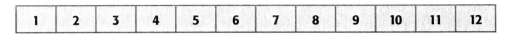

1	2	3	4	5	6	7	8	9	10	11	12

On the teacher's signal, students place all twelve of their markers on whichever numbers they like. It is acceptable to put more than one marker on one number and to leave numbers empty. The teacher then rolls a pair of dice. If a student has a marker on the sum of the two dice, she can remove the marker. If there is more than one marker on that number, only *one* marker can be removed. The game continues until one student has removed *all* her markers and is declared the winner.

After playing a game together as a class, students clear their boards and pair off. Each pair of students receives two dice and plays again, now one against the other. Allow students to play multiple rounds. The teacher moves around the room, listening to the conversations. He will notice that over time the students figure out the strategy for getting their markers off the board as quickly as possible.

The teacher saves a few minutes at the end of class to debrief and help students make connections between the game and probability theory (CCSS: Math.7.PS.6). Of course, they *all* will want to keep playing. Pose the question, "What is your best guess at a strategy for placing your markers so that you will be able to remove them first and win the game?"

Source: Lesson plan–roller derby (n.d.)

Team Rhythmic Dictation *(Music)*

For this activity, split the students into equal-sized teams of eight to ten students. Give group members blank sheets of white paper and ask students to draw on each sheet of paper the note values that you specify (one note per sheet). The notes should be large enough to fill an 8½ × 11 paper. The notes created should be a mix of whole, half, quarter, eighth, and sixteenth notes and there should be multiples of each note.

The teacher then plays for the teams a rhythmic pattern. Each team must arrange themselves in the proper order to represent the pattern that is played. The students should hold their sheet of paper in front of their chest and make sure that their rhythm pattern goes from left to right as though it were sheet music being read. If more than one measure is played, extra students should stand sideways to represent the bar lines. Each team that correctly represents the rhythm pattern receives one point. Play the pattern for the teams up to three times so that they can check for accuracy.

Source: Wickham (2009)

Dynamic Duos
(Physical Education)

This activity develops locomotor skills and body awareness and reinforces the importance of working collaboratively. Discuss with the students the need to be aware of their bodies and safe movement in an area. Select students to model the locomotor skills of skipping, hopping, jogging, jumping, lunging, sliding, and galloping.

When the music begins, the students move around performing the locomotor skill designated by the teacher. After a short time, the teacher stops the music and calls out a concept. For example, the concept might be a shape (square, circle, triangle), a specific letter of the alphabet in upper or lower case, a cardinal number from one to nine (for older students, numbers above nine), words and their opposites (wide, narrow, crooked, straight, over, under, small, big, above, below). When the music stops, each student quickly finds a nearby partner and they create the concept with their bodies.

Once the teacher has visually checked all the partners, the students separate, find a safe personal space, and get ready to move. The teacher calls out a different locomotor skill and the music begins. When the music stops, a new concept is called out. Students partner and create the concept.

By observing the students' interaction, the teacher can see which students might need additional help performing specific locomotor skills, understanding specific concepts or shapes, or realizing the importance of working well together.

Something's Fishy in Bio Class
(Science: Biology)

Can't afford to take your students to visit a world-class aquarium but want them to understand how adaptations allow species to survive in different habitats? By tapping into technology, students can find this out firsthand. Using the link to Chicago's Shedd Aquarium website (http://sea.sheddaquarium.org/sea/buildafish/flash.html), students build their own fish, choosing body type, mouth, and coloration. Once the fish has been created, it is released into the reef to eat or be eaten. This activity would be appropriate as a center for students to use during down time or as a way to introduce students to the purpose of adaptations and survival of the fittest.

Innovation *(Science: Chemistry)*

The NOVA Teachers site from PBS at http://www.pbs.org/wgbh/nova/education/resources/subject.html has a baker's dozen of subjects listed with a number of activities within each category. The activities include a teacher's guide, viewing ideas if there is a video clip attached, classroom activities, ideas from teachers, interactives for students, and related NOVA resources. The activities are highly engaging, have explicit instructions, yet can be easily modified to tailor-fit a classroom teacher's specific objectives. The topics are at the middle and high school level and range in length from a part of a class period to two class periods; most of them take one class period. The wide range of topics include absolute zero, microbes, the creation through chemistry of artificial gems, and the chemistry of plants.

A listing of chemistry activities can be found at the NOVA link on the Public Broadcasting Service website: http://www.pbs.org/wgbh/nova/education/resources/subj_02_03.html.

Parents and Daughters
(Science: Earth Science)

Major concepts like understanding Earth's geological history and determining the age of rocks are often difficult for students to fathom. This activity is appropriate when students have to study the concept of radioactive decay and half-life. As a prerequisite for this activity, students should be familiar with content-related terms (half-life, radioactive decay, parent element, daughter element) and the procedure geologists use to date the age of rocks. To make these concepts more real for students, the teacher sets up a simulation using popcorn as the medium. Unpopped kernels are labeled "parent" kernels. Heating the kernels begins the simulated radioactive decay and produces popped or "daughter" corn. The half-life of the kernel material is the time necessary for half of the unpopped kernels to become popped corn.

Each team is given one minibag of microwave popcorn. Teams are assigned different microwave popping times and label their bag with those times: 10 seconds, 20 seconds, 30 seconds, 40 seconds, 50 seconds, and 60 seconds. In sequential order beginning with 10 seconds, each team places its bag in the microwave and sets the timer for 2 minutes. At the sound of the first pop, students use a stopwatch to count off the number of seconds written on the bag. After that time has expired, they stop the microwave and remove the bag.

The teams open their bags and count the number of unpopped kernels (parent element) and the number of popped corns (daughter element) in the bag. The numbers for each team are recorded. Next, each team calculates the percentage of both unpopped kernels and popped corn. To do this, students count all of the unpopped and popped pieces to obtain the total number of kernels in the bag and then divide the number of unpopped kernels by the total number of kernels. The team uses the same process to find the percentage of the daughter element.

Students use the data to create a graph. The horizontal axis represents time, from 0 to 60 seconds. The vertical axis displays the percentage of material in each group's bag. Each team records its data on the graph. Students plot the curve of percentages of unpopped kernels in all bags. This curve shows the decay of the parent element or unpopped kernels over time. Next, they plot percentages of popped corn in each bag. The teacher asks questions like, "As the percentage of parent kernels gets smaller over time, what happens to the percentage of daughter popcorn?"

When the data are plotted, the two curves should intersect on the graph very near the 50 percent line on the vertical axis. Students might query, "What is the corresponding point on the horizontal axis, which represents time?" Students discover that this point represents the half-life of the kernel-popcorn material.

Using that graph, the teacher has the students make predictions. "If the kernel-popcorn material were rock, what would an ice core containing layers tell you about the age of other materials in that core? What would be the age of a layer containing 20 percent popped popcorn? What would be the age of a layer containing 80 percent popped popcorn?"

Source: Welch, Dunbar, McIntosh, & Heizler (2009)

Up, Up and Away
(Science: Physics)

When studying fluid dynamics in physics, students may have difficulty understanding the relevancy of the learning. Fluid dynamics has a wide range of applications, one of which is the physics of aerodynamics and flight, specifically calculating forces on aircraft. Using students' knowledge of Archimedes' principle, Bernoulli's principle, and air resistance or friction, the class can discuss possible designs for paper airplanes. Looking to create a paper airplane that will stay aloft the longest, students will design, build, and throw paper airplanes in a competition.

The teacher distributes pieces of paper of different weights, thicknesses, and finishes. Also available to students are supplies such as scissors, glue, tape, staples, and paper clips. Using the materials provided, each student designs an airplane that will stay airborne for the longest possible time.

Once the airplanes are constructed, the competition begins. On the day of the contest, students assemble outside on a playing field or inside in the gymnasium or other large area. Designate one student to time each student's plane as it is thrown. Record the times. Once all students have completed their first run, the entire class examines the plane that stayed aloft the longest. Together, they discuss the reasons why that specific plane flew the longest. Using that information, students redesign their planes. In the second round of the competition, students relaunch their planes, again timing the flights.

As a concluding activity, have students compare and contrast the designs and flight times. In a written format or in a class discussion, decide what made the best design and why.

To follow up, type "paper airplane designs" in the search box of a search engine. Students will find a number of sites where they can compare their designs to those on the Internet. Have students consider which designs are the most aerodynamic and the reasons why.

Source: Stewart (n.d.)

If ... , Then ...
(Social Studies: Economics)

Children's literature is a fabulous way to introduce serious topics in a fun way that is relevant to students' lives. In this primary-grade lesson, students explore the differences between cause and effect, wants and needs, goods and services, using Laura Numeroff's book *If You Give a Mouse a Cookie.*

Introduce to students cause-and-effect statements (CCSS: ELA. RI.3.3). Ask the students if they have ever heard statements like "If you finish your dinner (cause), you can have dessert (effect)," "If you help to pick up the toys (cause), we can go to your cousins' house (effect)," or "If you behave properly (cause), you can have an extra thirty minutes of media time (effect)." These are cause-and-effect statements. Have the students give some that they may have heard or said, using the format "If you _____, then _____."

Read the book *If You Give a Mouse a Cookie* and have students identify the cause-and-effect statements.

Next, explain the difference between a good and a service. A good is something that can be touched and used. A service is something that someone does for you. Identify the goods and services that the mouse wanted in the story. Discuss what goods and services students might want.

Explore the differences between a want and a need. A want is something that you would like to have but do not need for survival. Wants are unlimited; the list can go on forever. A need is something that is essential for survival: basic shelter, enough food and water to maintain health, basic health care and hygiene products, and clothing so that one is comfortable and appropriately dressed.

Once the mouse's wants and needs have been explored, give the students a sentence starter like "If you give the teacher a book, then she would _____." Ask students to generate fifteen to twenty cause-and-effect statements that follow this format; record those statements on chart paper. Then read the story again. The students can decide if the statements are goods or services, wants or needs. The students and/or the teacher can keyboard the statements, each on a separate page. The students can illustrate the completed story and share it with another class or group.

As an extension, students can create their own stories starring themselves and illustrate and bind them to share with parents or friends. Each story would use cause and effect statements following the model of *If You Give a Mouse a Cookie*. The students' stories would include specific wants and needs as well as goods and services. To assess students, this rubric might be helpful (see over):

	Getting Started	**Almost There**	**Got It**	**Wow!**
The story has at least 15 cause-and-effect sentences.	0 to 6 cause-and-effect statements	7 to 14 cause-and-effect statements	15 cause-and-effect statements	More than 15 cause-and-effect statements
Includes an illustration or image for each of the 15 statements	0 to 6 illustrations or images	7 to 14 illustrations or images	15 illustrations or images	More than 15 illustrations or images
Presentation	The story rarely follows the pattern and often does not make sense. The images do not go along with the text.	The story does not always follow the pattern and make sense. The images do not illustrate the text well.	The story generally follows the pattern and makes sense. The images go along with the text.	Everything works! The story follows the pattern and makes sense. The images go along well with the text.
Mechanics	Many spelling, capitalization, and grammar errors	Some spelling, capitalization, and grammar errors	Few, if any, spelling, capitalization, and grammar errors	Spelling, capitalization, and grammar are error-free
The story has a final chapter defining the terms "cause and effect," "goods and services," "wants and needs"	Few of the definitions are correct	Most of the definitions are correct	The definitions are correct	All of the definitions are correct and supported by examples from the text

Source: Suiter (n.d.)

I've Been Everywhere, Man
(Social Studies: Geography)

Geography is known as the "why of where." Before students can get to that point of understanding, it is important for them to understand their place in the world through geography. For students with a limited experiential background, this can be a real challenge. Music teachers, mathematics teachers, and the school librarian can collaborate with the social studies teacher to carry out *I've Been Everywhere, Man*. For success, students should be pretaught or have a grasp of basic map skills.

Begin by playing the song "I've Been Everywhere" by Johnny Cash for the students. Students should have a lyric sheet so that they can follow along. Divide the students into small groups. Groups first find on a map each of the places the hitchhiker visited. The school librarian could introduce the students to the use of an atlas or computer mapping software. As students locate each of the cities from the song, they note the latitude and longitude. Next students estimate the mileage of the total journey and the approximate time that it would take a hitchhiker to complete the trip. Students justify their thinking behind the calculation. They then compare that calculation to what they might find using computer mapping software. Each group is then charged to find a "better" way to map out the trip in order for the hitchhiker to save time and money. Group members cite a key fact for each of the locations—why would the hitchhiker want to go to each of the cities? Student groups present their findings to the entire class.

As an extension activity, each group selects and substitutes different locations in place of those in the original song. Students could perform the song and share the map of their places of interest with others.

iCivics: Doing Our Civic Duty
(Social Studies: Government/ Political Science)

Highly interactive and engaging, *iCivics* is an interactive website that allows students to play video games and participate in webquests. Through these games, students better understand how to participate in the government process. The video games are free and can be played by individual students or as a whole class using a projector and whiteboard. The site's games and webquests are focused on different aspects of federal government—Citizenship and Participation, Constitution and Bill of Rights, Budgeting, Foreign Policy and National Defense, Separation of Powers, and the Legislative, Executive and Judicial Branches. The *iCivics* video games are standards-aligned and have a large bank of teacher supplemental materials.

iCivics was founded by Supreme Court Justice Sandra Day O'Connor with the intention of increasing students' civic knowledge and participation and is supported and endorsed by a number of organizations, including the American Bar Association, the Center for Civic Education, Citizenship Counts, the National Constitution Center, and Street Law.

As students play the games they earn points that they can spend on one of the impact projects listed on the *iCivics* site. An impact project is a community-service project that has been established by students from different parts of the country. Students designate their earned points for a specific project. They can write a post advocating for their chosen project and persuade other students to vote for the same project. Quarterly, the impact project that earns the most points is awarded $1,000 by *iCivics*. Students can help others and learn. For a teen this is tough to top.

Source: iCivics (n.d.)

Elevator Speech
(Social Studies: History)

An elevator speech or elevator pitch is a short summary used to quickly and succinctly define something. *Elevator Speech* is so named because a person should be able to deliver the summary in the time span of an elevator ride, from thirty seconds to two minutes. An elevator speech can be presented in oral, written, and/or video format.

In a unit regarding landmark Supreme Court cases (CCSS: WHST.11.1), trios of students are assigned to a specific case. Here is a list of suggested cases:

- *Marbury v. Madison*
- *McCulloch v. Maryland*
- *Gibbons v. Ogden*
- *Dred Scott v. Sandford*
- *Plessy v. Ferguson*
- *Schenck v. US*
- *Korematsu v. US*
- *Map v. Ohio*
- *Gideon v. Wainwright*
- *Escobedo v. Illinois*
- *Miranda v. Arizona*
- *Tinker v. Des Moines*

- *Roe v. Wade*
- *US v. Nixon*
- *Regents of University of California v. Bakke*
- *New Jersey v. TLO*
- *Texas v. Johnson*
- *Hazelwood v. Kuhlmeier*
- *Miller v. Alabama*

For each case, two of the students in each trio take opposite sides, research the arguments, and develop an elevator speech advocating for their position. The third student takes on the role of a Supreme Court justice, researching the final decision and the reason for such a decision. The three elevator speeches are presented to the rest of the class. The teacher facilitates the conversation following the speeches, focusing on the impact of the decision and the implications for US citizens today.

Generations and Demographics
(Social Studies: Sociology)

Sociology is the study of people and relationships through the examination of social dynamics and human behavior. The study of sociology allows students to investigate how people's age, sex, race, ethnicity, and religious background influence their reaction to or perception of different issues. The students are presented with a variety of questions, statements, and images that cover different issues and ideas—the economy, health care, gun control, same-sex marriage, conflict around the world, even different facets of pop culture such as fashion, movies, and music. Ask students for their reactions. Choose a recorder to list the responses with demographics noted, if possible.

Next, divide the class into smaller groups. Each group develops a hypothesis as to how different generations (preteens, twenty-somethings, parents, grandparents) or different demographics of people might respond to the same images and questions.

The group then shares its hypothesis with classmates and, through feedback, refines it. The group tests its hypothesis by meeting with a number of representatives from the different groups and recording their responses. The student groups report back to the entire class, sharing their findings. Conclusions are formed and whole-class dialogue commences.

Source: Eblin (n.d.)

Glogster *(Technology)*

For a unit of study on a specified topic in any content area, students would enjoy using technology to create a Glogster (CCSS: WHST.9.6). Glogsters are 21st-century digital posters that can be created through the use of edu.glogster.com. The content of the poster varies depending upon the student topic. The teacher creates a class account at edu.glogster.com and receives up to fifty free student accounts. The directions to create a Glogster are fairly straightforward for students and teachers to follow. When creating their poster, students can import graphics, text, images, video, and sound. Students can go in and out of the program, saving and editing the Glogster until they are satisfied with the final product. At that point, the Glogster can be published to a larger audience. Students are able to express their creativity, knowledge, ideas, and skills. To grade a Glogster, consider using a rubric like the one below.

	Beginning	Developing	Accomplished	Exemplary
Glogster has at least 10 facts about specific topic	0 to 4 facts Does not lead the viewer to an understanding of the concept being depicted	5 to 8 facts May focus on trivial facts that do not help the viewer understand the topic	9 to 10 facts Leads the viewer to an understanding of the topic	More than 10 facts Facts are specific, in depth, and appropriate; not trivial information
Includes a minimum of 3 graphics	0 to 1 graphic	2 graphics	3 graphics	More than 3 graphics, at least one of which is animated
Includes a minimum of 3 text boxes	0 to 1 text box	2 text boxes	3 text boxes	More than 3 text boxes
Includes a minimum of 3 imported images	0 to 1 image	2 images	3 images	More than 3 images

Continued

	Beginning	Developing	Accomplished	Exemplary
Visually pleasing	Viewer is distracted by the presentation and can only get a limited understanding of topic	Font size may not be appropriate; background, visuals, and/or graphics are distracting. Viewer gets some of the key elements of the topic	Good use of color, font size, and information. Viewer can get a complete understanding of topic	Everything works! The topic's images and graphics coordinate with the background to give the viewer a well-rounded exposure to the content, complete and specific
Mechanics	Many spelling, capitalization, and grammar errors	Some spelling, capitalization, and grammar errors	Few spelling, capitalization, and grammar errors	Spelling, capitalization, and grammar are error-free

Note: There are many Glogster examples on the website. It is imperative that teachers screen these to ensure that the content is appropriate to use as a classroom model.

The Art of the Ball Toss
(variation of Beach Ball Review)
(Visual Art)

This activity is a great way to have a little fun and expend some energy! Purchase an inflatable or rubber ball and, with a permanent marker, carefully draw lines around the circumference bisecting the sphere and creating a number of sections. In each section created, print a question that relates to the art work that is being discussed and/or reviewed.

- What style does the artist use?
- How does this work of art make you feel?

- If you were the artist, what different materials might you use?
- What is the title of the piece and what is the meaning behind the title?
- Did the author intend for the viewer to find a deeper meaning in the work?
- Compare and contrast this work with ...

Students stand in a circle in an open area and gently toss the ball to someone in the circle. The student who catches it finds the question that is under her right thumb, reads the question, and responds. The teacher or other students can probe and ask follow-up questions before the student tosses the ball to a different person in the circle. Play continues as time allows or until all questions are answered.

Chapter 11

What Comes Next?

"The secret of getting ahead is getting started. The secret of getting started is breaking your complex overwhelming tasks into small manageable tasks, and then starting on the first one."

—Mark Twain

Excited about getting started? Ready to take the first steps? Do as Mark Twain suggests and begin to think about how to break the whole idea of seriously fun instruction into small manageable tasks. In an earlier chapter, we suggested that the step before doing is thinking. Reflection allows you to specifically identify the elements of a seriously fun classroom and determine which of these elements are already in place.

Think back to how this book began. A seriously fun classroom clearly connects to content while at the same time it engages and motivates students. Seriously fun strategies and activities are purposefully designed to hit upon elements of a 21st-century classroom and address the Common Core State Standards. A seriously fun classroom encourages students to make choices, collaborate with each other, make decisions, and use higher-level thinking, all while they are working on open-ended, relevant problems. Of course, when there is movement, laughter, humor, and fun in the activity, everyone wins! Not all of the elements need to be present in every activity, but when that happens, it is like hitting the jackpot. As you review your lessons and the activities and strategies in each, hold them up against the checklist of elements found in a seriously fun classroom provided in Chapter 1. The strategies and activities that have these elements are the keepers. Give yourself a pat on the back for a great start.

We would suggest that you start small. Most teachers are already doing some seriously fun work and are too busy to throw out everything that has been previously completed and start from scratch. Examine an upcoming lesson or unit of instruction and consider what you might include in order to add an element of fun. In Appendix D you'll find sample lesson plans. Use them as templates that *you* embellish with *your* work and ideas. Add the little extras that move you toward your goal of achieving a seriously fun classroom.

Remember, Mr. Serious Fun did not walk into the classroom on Day 1 and have everything just the way he wanted it. He continually reflects upon his practice and makes the changes that are necessary to take teaching and learning to the next level. The best professionals always tweak and fuss with lessons, improving them or modifying them to best fit the needs of their students. We know that by considering some of the suggestions outlined in *Serious Fun*, you will move your students closer to the skill set that is required of 21st-century citizens while addressing the rigor of the Common Core.

Let's spend a little more time investigating the ten tips for serious fun listed in Chapter 1.

Select fun activities that have essential content and skills as the primary focus. As lessons are designed, time and effort are best invested in linking rigorous academic content and skill work with fun and humor. The novelty of incorporating humor and fun into the lessons allows your students' brains to more readily latch on to new learning. The likelihood of retention is increased whenever students are actively engaged in their work.

Expect a little chaos. When we play and have fun, things can get a little messy. When lessons are effectively structured, the use of humor and fun in the classroom raises the excitement level while improving the focus of student conversation, collaboration. and competition. Expect that initially there may be an increase in transition times and noise level. To establish good classroom management, be sure that students learn the procedures and expectations before any activity is undertaken so that they clearly understand the desired behaviors. Monitor what is happening and be prepared to make adjustments, sometimes on the fly.

Rigor should be the number one priority of instruction. High standards are the business of school. Every activity, in every classroom, every day must focus on successful student attainment of content and skill standards found in the CCSS or in state and local standards. Using humor and fun is not an excuse for decreasing academic rigor. As you have read, a seriously fun classroom can actually be more rigorous in that it honors what we know about how to maximize learning. Play can actually look a lot like work.

Invite change. Experienced and novice educators alike may find the integration of fun activities and the use of humor in instruction a departure from the known. They therefore present a challenge. If you're feeling challenged, you're probably going through some change. When you reflect at the conclusion of the lesson, jot down your ideas and thoughts about how you can make positive changes for the next time. Think back to Chapter 3 and Mr. Serious Fun's experience with *Snowball Review*. The strategy didn't go well initially. As a matter of fact, he might even have called it a disaster. But after reflecting on the activity, he thought about how to make it work better for his students. He made changes, willingly and without hesitation. The next time he tried the activity, it was *much* more successful. Recall, as well, that Mr. SF is *still* working on making things better.

Overtly observe student engagement and interest. According to Madeline Hunter, overt active participation is essential to good instruction. When students play while learning, the teacher can directly hear students' thoughts about the content and skill and get a better understanding of the thinking that helped them to reach a particular conclusion. The activities in a seriously fun classroom are opportunities for formative assessment. Many of the strategies have built-in assessment characteristics. Through observation of students engaged in the suggested activities, teachers can really get a handle on what students understand. Using that information, the teacher can think about the next lesson and what needs to be done so that all students "get it." The next step may require reviewing material, providing on-the-spot help for a few students, or moving ahead. When observing or collecting written work, a teacher can make an informed decision about the next best steps.

Unexpected learnings *will* occur. When students participate in learning activities that have an element of fun, there will be some surprises. And almost all of them are good. There is a different type of thinking required. Students are exploring and discovering, and it is not uncommon to hear "Wow, now I get it!" Seriously fun activities and strategies also allow students to tap into a different part of their brain to solve problems. Serious fun often allows students who might not shine in a "read-the-text-listen-to-the-lecture-do-the-homework-take-the-test" classroom to step forward. Novel solutions to problems present themselves due to the out-of-the-box thinking that is encouraged by seriously fun activities.

Systemically use humor and fun in *all* content areas. Consistency in teaching practices both vertically and horizontally is one of the best ways to make the learning environment the best it can be. Ideally, moving toward a seriously fun classroom is accomplished more easily when educators collaborate, working with their teammates, grade-level partners, or colleagues in the entire school. The energy level increases with collaboration. When humor and fun pervade all content areas, they create a positive climate for student learning. Students are excited about going to class as they wonder what they'll be learning next. There is joy in the classroom and success reigns!

Find opportunities for students to work collaboratively and have fun together. Humans enjoy working hard with friends and colleagues to conquer challenges and achieve a common goal. Making this process fun and inviting will lead to real success. Consider athletes on a sports team. They work hard, push each other, offer encouragement, and eagerly take on additional challenges. They don't quit. They share a camaraderie and a team focus on the end goal—winning. This feeling can translate to a classroom setting. If the context of the classroom is inviting, students want to be there. And there is nothing more appealing than having fun with others. If lessons are structured so that students are challenged to think, question, and work together, focused on the goal of learning, then they will work hard. Hard work is expected from students in school but that does not preclude them from having fun. As humans, we tend to be very creative when we're playing. For many of us, the old adage "Plays well with others" says it all.

Use what you already have. Revel in what works now and take advantage of your successes from the past. Many of your lessons can be reworked with minimal effort to infuse humor and fun into the learning environment. Just because it didn't work before doesn't mean it can't work now. The more time and effort invested in reflecting on and reworking what you have already done, the bigger the payback can be. Just ask Mr. Serious Fun.

Next steps? There is no doubt that working as an educator in the 21st-century is a great challenge. Now is the time to meet and exceed that challenge by making school a seriously fun place to be. Through the use of laughter, play, humor, and fun in every classroom, our schools will become places students *want* to be, not *have* to be.

Most of *Serious Fun* has focused on the use of strategies by teachers at all grade levels in a wide variety of content areas. Educators in leadership roles can also use these strategies effectively in their work with adults. Principals can incorporate some of the suggested activities as they plan for meetings with teachers and parents. They may choose to use this book as a school-wide book study. Leaders might use the first chapter to begin a conversation about the need for humor and play in the classroom and then have teachers select a couple of strategies to use in their lessons over the following week. At the next meeting, or through Skype, e-mail conferences, and team meetings, teachers can reflect on and discuss what worked and what didn't and how to adapt the strategy or activity to each teacher's specific group of students.

The authors work with many educators to foster serious fun in the classroom. At the end of those professional development opportunities, an evaluation is used that asks attendees to choose from a list of words that they feel best describe their learning that day. The list includes words such as "creativity," "curiosity," "passion," and "success." Two words that are among the most often chosen are "fun" and "relevant." That is very telling. In order to be effective, learning should be relevant, and apparently, to a number of educators, it's important that learning has an element of fun. Think about what your students would say about *your* lessons. Would "fun" and "relevant" be *their* top choices?

In order for our students to be successful in the future, schools can no longer primarily be "about the math" (or the social studies or any content area of your choice). Schools' number one focus must be on the future facing our young people. Their lives, personally and professionally, will be filled with problem solving, collaboration, and creativity. For them to be successful, the skills needed will be different from those in the past. Children who spend a week in class learning a specific, discrete piece of content at the expense of other 21st-century skills may find themselves lagging behind, woefully underprepared for college and/or the world of work. In the 21st century, discrete pieces of information, such as basic formulas, grammar rules, and names, dates, and places, are readily available via a wealth of resources, like the Internet. Skills such as problem solving and collaboration cannot be honed with a quick Google search. These skills must be a serious focus of what happens in our classrooms *every* day.

So what's next as you move forward with serious fun in *your* classroom? We hope this book has started you thinking about your work, the crucial role fun plays in making learning relevant and successful, and how *you* can make that happen in *your* classroom. As you take those next steps, you are likely to find more seriously fun strategies; please let us know. And if you find yourself with wonderful, new adaptations to the strategies in this book, it is important to share those, as well. Subsequent editions and/or supplements could include *your* name.

In one of our favorite songs from the 1970s, Tower of Power exclaimed, "You ought to be havin' fun." It is our belief that when the classroom environment is emotionally charged in positive ways, highly engaging, and filled with fun, two things are sure to be true. First, the teacher has worked incredibly long and hard to make this happen, and secondly, students are learning and having the time of their lives, constantly asking for more! W.B. Yeats once said that our classrooms should not be the filling of buckets but the lighting of fires. Rather than just cramming more and more information into students' brains, let's consciously think about how to kindle a child's *love* for learning. Students in a seriously fun classroom will have their curiosity fueled, their passion sparked, and their learning ignited. Students will be eager to walk into your seriously fun classroom every single day—because life (and school) should be fun ... seriously!

Bibliography

Appleton, V. (1910). *Tom Swift and his airship*. New York, NY: Grosset & Dunlap.

Bafile, C. (2000, February 7). Education world: A "real-life fair" shows kids the real deal about careers. *Education World*. Retrieved from http://www.educationworld.com/a_curr/curr196.shtml.

Blanchard, K. H., & Barrett, C. (2010). *Lead with LUV: A different way to create real success*. Upper Saddle River, NJ: FT Press.

Bloom, B. S. (1956). *Taxonomy of educational objectives*. New York: Longmans, Green.

BrainyWeightLoss. (2013). *Physical benefits of laughter therapy*. Retrieved from http://www.brainyweightloss.com/physical-benefits-of-laughter.html#axzz23RfCuyxv.

Brewer, C. (1995). Music and Learning: Integrating music in the classroom. *Johns Hopkins University School of Education*. Retrieved from http://education.jhu.edu/PD/newhorizons/strategies/topics/Arts%20in%20Education/brewer.htm.

Casserly, M. (2012). Dream companies for the Class of 2012: Everybody wants to work at Google. *Forbes*. Retrieved from http://www.forbes.com/sites/meghancasserly/2012/05/11/dream-companies-for-class-2012-everybody-wants-to-work-at-google/2/.

Chang, K. (2011, January 17). Bending and stretching classroom lessons to make math inspire. *New York Times*.

Cohen, P. (1995). Understanding the brain: Educators seek to apply brain research. *Education Update, 37*(7), 1.

Colmenares, C. (2005, June 10). No joke: Study finds laughing can burn calories. *Vanderbilt University Medical Center*. Retrieved from http://www.mc.vanderbilt.edu/reporter/index.html?ID=4030.

Colorado Department of Education. (2010). *Instructional practices that make a difference*. Retrieved from http://www.cde.state.co.us/.../EdMeetings_12Dec2010_Anticipator.

Common Core State Standards Initiative (CCSSI). (2010). Retrieved from http://www.corestandards.org/.

Csikszentmihalyi, M., & Csikszentmihalyi, I. S. (1988). *Optimal experience: Psychological studies of flow in consciousness*. Cambridge, UK: Cambridge University Press.

Dalgarno, B. (1998). Choosing learner activities for specific learning outcomes: A tool for constructivist computer assisted learning design. In C. McBeath and R. Atkinson (Eds.), *Planning for progress, partnership and profit*. Proceedings EdTech'98. Perth: Australian Society for Educational Technology. Retrieved from http://www.aset.org.au/confs/edtech98/pubs/articles/dalgarno.html.

Danforth, W. (n.d.). Nestlé© Purina pet care: Purina Dog Food, Cat Food & more. Nestle©Purina.com. Retrieved from http://www.nestlepurina.com/danforth.aspx.

Dr. Seuss [Theodor Geisel]. (1990). *Oh, the places you'll go!* New York: Random House.

Dugdale, D. C. (2011, August 5). Antigen: Medline Plus Medical Encyclopedia. National Library of Medicine, National Institutes of Health. Retrieved from http://www.nlm.nih.gov/medlineplus/ency/article/002224.htm.

Eblin, J. (n.d.). High school sociology activities. *eHow.com*. Retrieved April 15, 2013, from http://www.ehow.com/list_6580994_high-school-sociology-activities.html.

Faulkner, B. (2012). The magnetism of language: Parts of speech, poetry, and word play—*ReadWriteThink*. Retrieved April 15, 2013, from http://www.readwritethink.org/classroom-resources/lesson-plans/magnetism-language-parts-speech-1058.html?tab=4#tabs.

Freiberg, K., & Freiberg, J. (1998). *Nuts! Southwest Airlines' crazy recipe for business and personal success*. Austin, TX: Bard Books.

Fun Theory. (2012). Retrieved from http://thefuntheory.com.

Gardner, H. (1983). *Frames of mind: The theory of multiple intelligences*. New York: Basic Books.

Gates, D. (n.d.). Math Munchers. *MrGym.com*. Retrieved April 15, 2013, from http://mrgym.com/Cooperatives/Math_Munchers.htm.

Gogolla, N. et al. (2009, September 9). The amygdala's role in learning, memory, social intelligence, criminal behavior, mood disorders and especially the retention of traumatic memories in adult PTSD. *Impact: SLA Leadership & Management Division Blog*. Retrieved from http://sla-divisions.typepad.com/dbio/2009/09/the-amygdalas-role-in-learning-memory-social-intelligence-criminal-behavior-mood-disorders-and-espec.html.

Good, T. L. (2008). Students as social beings. *21st century education: A reference handbook*. Los Angeles, CA: Sage.

Hannaford, C. (1995). *Smart moves: Why learning is not all in your head*. Arlington, VA: Great Ocean.

Harris, M. (2009). *Music and the young mind: Enhancing brain development and engaging learning*. Lanham, MD: Rowman & Littlefield Publishers, Inc.

Harrison, C. (n.d.). Always write: My writer's notebook challenge for December! *Always Write: My Teacher/Trainer Homepage*. Retrieved April 15, 2013, from http://corbettharrison.com/GT/Tom-Swift.htm.

Havighurst, R., & Davis, A. (1943). Child socialization in the school. *Review of Educational Research, 13*(1), 29.

Hunter, M. (1982). *Mastery teaching*. Thousand Oaks, CA: Corwin Press.

iCivics. (n.d.). Retrieved April 15, 2013, from http://www.icivics.org/.

Improbable Research. (2012). Retrieved from http://www.improbable.com/ig/2012.

Jensen, E. (2005). *Teaching with the brain in mind* (2nd ed.). Alexandria, VA: ASCD.

Kagan, S., & Kagan, M. (2009). *Kagan cooperative learning*. San Clemente, CA: Kagan.

Kearsley, G., & Shneiderman, B. (1999). *Engagement theory: A framework for technology-based teaching and learning*. Retrieved from http://home.sprynet.com/~gkearsley/engage.htm.

Kohn, A. (2004, September 15). Feel-bad education: The cult of rigor and the loss of joy. *Education Week, 24*(3), 36, 44.

Lead with LUV: Treating people right. (n.d.). *YouTube*. Retrieved from http://www.youtube.com/watch?v=VVM0xMQ0LEQ&feature=relmfu.

Lesson plan–roller derby. (n.d.). *Electronic Flip*. Retrieved April 15, 2013, from http://mrflip.com/teach/uteach-examples/full/Communication/Roller%20Derby.html.

Levering, R., & Moskowitz, M. (2012). 100 best companies to work for 2012. *Great Place to Work Institute*. Retrieved from http://www.greatplacetowork.com/best-companies/100-best-companies-to-work-for.

Loomans, D., & Kolberg, K. (2002). *The laughing classroom: Everyone's guide to teaching with humor and play*. Tiburon, CA: H. J. Kramer. (Originally published 1993.)

Lyman, F. (1981). The responsive classroom discussion: The inclusion of all students. *Mainstreaming Digest*. College Park: University of Maryland.

Marzano, R. J. (2004). *Building background knowledge for academic achievement*. Alexandria, VA: ASCD.

Marzano, R. J., Pickering, D., & Pollock, J. E. (2001). Applying the research on instruction. *Classroom instruction that works: Research-based strategies for increasing student achievement* (p. 7). Alexandria, VA: ASCD.

Metcalf, C. W., & Felible, R. (1992). *Lighten up: Survival skills for people under pressure*. Reading, MA: Addison-Wesley.

Newell, P. (1912). "The rocket book." *Library of Congress*. Retrieved from http://read.gov/books/rocket.html and http://www.read.gov/books/pageturner/2003juv23925/#page/4/mode/2up.

Nolte, C. (2008). Other fun in-class learning activities for marketing. *MarketingProfs*. Retrieved from http://www.marketingprofs.com/ea/qst_question.asp?qstID=21685#ixzz27Qy.

Ogle, D. (1986). K-W-L: A teaching model that develops active reading of expository text. *The Reading Teacher, 39*(6), 564–570.

The Partnership for 21st Century Skills (P21). (2008). *21st century skills, education & competitiveness: A resource and policy guide*. Tucson AZ: The Partnership for 21st Century Skills.

The Partnership for 21st Century Skills (P21). (n.d.). *Common core toolkit*. Retrieved from http://www.p21.org/tools-and-resources/publications/p21-common-core-toolkit.

Pfeffer, J., & Sutton, R. I. (2000). *The knowing-doing gap: How smart companies turn knowledge into action*. Boston: MA: Harvard Business School Press.

Philbrick, W. R. (1993). *Freak the mighty*. New York, NY: Blue Sky Press.

Scott, E. (2012, June 18). The benefit of laughter: How laughter can reduce stress and increase health. *Stress and stress management: Causes, symptoms, stress relief tips and stress tests*. Retrieved from http://stress.about.com/od/stresshealth/a/laughter.htm.

Short, K. G., Harste, J. C., & Burke, C. L. (1996). *Creating classrooms for authors and inquirers* (2nd ed.). Portsmouth, NH: Heinemann.

Six-Word Memoirs. (2012, December 5). *Wikipedia: The Free Encyclopedia*. Retrieved January 2, 2013, from http://en.wikipedia.org/w/index.php?title=Six-Word_Memoirs&oldid=526601648.

Smith, J. (2012, June 11). The best travel companies to work for. *Forbes*. Retrieved from http://www.forbes.com/sites/jacquelynsmith/2012/06/11/the-best-travel-companies-to-work-for/.

Smith, M., & Segal, J. (2012). Laughter is the best medicine: The health benefits of humor. *Helpguide helps you help yourself and others*. Retrieved from http://www.helpguide.org/life/humor_laughter_health.htm.

S.O.S. for Information Literacy. (n.d.). *Japanese business trip*. Retrieved April 15, 2013, from http://www.informationliteracy.org/plans/view/1935/back/0.

Stewart, L. (2012). Cartoon physics. *Education.com*. Retrieved from http://www.education.com/activity/article/Cartoon_Physics_high.

Stewart, L. (n.d.). Make a better paper airplane. *Education.com*. Retrieved April 13, 2013, from http://www.education.com/activity/article/Paper_Airplane_high/.

Straker, D. (n.d.). Quotes and quotations from the wise on all matters creative. *CreatingMinds*. Retrieved from http://creatingminds.org/quotes/challenge.htm.

Suiter, M. (n.d.). Lesson: Give a mouse a cookie. *Economic Education Web: EcEdWeb*. Retrieved April 15, 2013, from http://ecedweb.unomaha.edu/lessons/mouse.htm#.

Wagner, T. (2008). *The global achievement gap: Why even our best schools don't teach the new survival skills our children need—and what we can do about it*. New York, NY: Basic Books.

Wassermann, S. (1992). Serious play in the classroom: How messing around can win you the Nobel Prize. *Childhood Education, 68*(3), 133–139.

Welch, S., Dunbar, N., McIntosh, B., & Heizler, L. (2009). Dating popcorn. *Earth Science Week*. Retrieved April 13, 2013, from http://www.earthsciweek.org/forteachers/2009/DatingPopcorn_Feb_cont.html.

West, L. (2005). *Lessons in loyalty: How Southwest Airlines does it: An insider's view*. Dallas, TX: CornerStone Leadership Institute.

Wickham, N. (2009, February 9). Monday mailbag—Large group games. *Music Matters Blog*. Retrieved April 15, 2013, from http://musicmattersblog.com/2009/02/09/monday-mailbag-large-group-games/.

Willis, J. (2011). Big thinkers: Judy Willis on the science of learning. *YouTube*. Retrieved from http://www.youtube.com/watch?v=J6FqAiAbUFs.

Wright, T. (n.d.). Music and learning … A perfect match! *Songs for Teaching*. Retrieved from http://songsforteaching.net/music-and-learning.

Yankelovich, D. (1984). Science and the public process. *Issues in Science and Technology, 1*(1), 6–12.

Appendices

Strategies Chart

Chapters 4 through 9 of *Serious Fun* offer instructional strategies that provide teachers with multiple ways to make their classroom more seriously fun. These strategies are presented here in chart form as a quick reference guide. For more detailed directions on each strategy, please refer to the page number (#), found in the far right column.

You might want to bookmark this chart. Identify the strategies that look interesting, that would work for you and your students, or that seem like they just might be fun. Keep plenty of reflective notes so that you can tweak and customize the strategies to best fit your students' needs.

Key

Factor to seriously consider	Cost ($)	Teacher preparation time needed (T)	Classroom time needed (C)
Low (L)	Less than $1	Less than 5 minutes	Less than 5 minutes
Medium (M)	$1 to $5	5 to 15 minutes	5 to 10 minutes
High (H)	More than $5	More than 15 minutes	More than 10 minutes

- Costs are estimates and can vary. There may be more costs initially, but materials can be saved and reused, ultimately reducing the cost per use over time.
- Teacher preparation time will be longer the first time a strategy is prepared. Subsequent uses are highly likely to take less time.
- Because of the depth of spirited conversation that can result from students engaging in these seriously fun strategies, classroom time needed may vary.

Name of Strategy	Brief Description	$	T	C	#
2-1	• 2 key words/short phrases • 1 point to ponder	L	L	L to M	92
3-2-1	• 3 important learnings • 2 interesting ideas • 1 question I still have	L	L	L to M	92
5-3-1	• 5 new words/short phrases • 3 things to think about • 1 way this will help me	L	L	M	92
24/7	• Teams of students describe content in 24 seconds, then offer a 7-word summary/sentence	L	L	H	32
Aha! Slips	• Small slips of paper are given to students • Whenever they discover an interesting learning, they write it on an "Aha!" slip • These slips can be used in whatever fashion the teacher decides • See *Bag of Tricks*	L	M	M	93
Baggage Claim	• Students write responses to prompts on a luggage icon • They move around the room sharing info on bags, trading bags with partners • Students continue sharing and trading for a predetermined amount of time • Return bags to original owner	M	M	M	84
Bag of Tricks	• Each student decorates a paper lunch bag • As ideas are discovered (See *Aha! Slips*), they go into the bag • When directed or as review, students remove a slip from their bag and share in whatever fashion deemed appropriate	M	L	L to H	93
Beach Ball Review	• Students are arranged into circles and toss an inflated ball around • When the music stops, the person holding the ball shares a learning from the unit • Continue the process	M to H	L	L	94
Block Out	• Pairs or trios share a sheet of paper with boxes containing various prompts covered by sticky notes • First student removes a sticky note, uncovering a prompt • Student responds to the prompt and then passes the paper to the left or right • Continue until all boxes have been uncovered	L	M	M	59
Bright Idea	• Distribute paper with a graphic of a lightbulb • Use any time when students wish to jot down something of importance • Ask students to use this paper to do their homework • Variations: T-shirt, sneaker, bicycle, car; any icon that is relevant	L	L	L	94

Continued

Name of Strategy	Brief Description	$	T	C	#
Carousel	• Small groups write information pertinent to the heading on chart paper with a unique colored marker • Groups move in a clockwise direction to each of the other charts, one at a time, writing comments using their colored marker • Groups return to original station and engage in conversation about what they observed and learned	M	L	M to H	75
Classroom Contest	• Teacher chooses a content-related prompt • Students generate possible responses • Teacher reveals "right answers" from 10 to 1 • Students score points for matched responses	L	H	H	50
Color-Coding	• Teachers form groups of students using colored index cards or dots • Could also be used for differentiation	M	L	L	59
Consenso-gram	• Teacher writes a content-related statement on chart paper • Teacher labels the horizontal axis • Students place sticky notes above their choice • Final product resembles a bar graph	M	M	M	50
Defend or Dispute	• Teacher chooses a content-related statement that requires students to make a judgment • Students choose a side • Opposing pairs debate	L	L	M	52
Exit Card/ Ticket Out the Door	• Students record a key idea from the day's learning on an index card • As a pass to leave the room, they hand the cards to the teacher, who can use them as appropriate	M	L	L	95
Exquisite Corpse	• A student writes a content-related statement at the top of a sheet of paper • The paper is passed from one team member to the next, each student adding a sentence or illustration • Each person sees *only* the entry immediately preceding his; all other previous entries are hidden from view • Once everyone has had a turn, *all* entries are reviewed by the team and discussed	L	L	M to H	60
Facebook Pages	• Students list the elements of a Facebook page for a person they are studying • Students conduct research on the person • Students create a fake Facebook page for the person, including profile picture, cover photo, information that the person would probably have recorded, the person's friends, likes, photos, maps, timeline, being sure to stay in character • The finished files can be downloaded to the class's webpage	L	M	M to H	33

Continued

Name of Strategy	Brief Description	$	T	C	#
Final Word	• One student in a group responds first to a teacher-generated prompt • Everyone else, in turn, responds while the first person listens only • The conversation returns to the first student who gets the final word • Continue the process	L	L	M to H	76
Find Someone Who	• Students/staff each have a handout with a list of prompts, questions, or statements • Students/staff move around the room finding different classmates/colleagues to respond to the prompts	L	M	M to H	61
First Word	• Students make acronyms for content-related topics as a way to prepare for a lesson	L	L	M	52
Focused Reading	• A means to give students a purpose for reading • Example: Student responds after reading—one thing I *do* know; one thing I *think* I know; one thing I *don't* know	L	L	L	95
For the Role of…	• When it's time to assign roles/tasks for students, make a fun choice, like "the person who lives closest to the school"	L	L	L	62
Four Corners	• Content-related prompts are posted in each corner of the room • Students choose to go to one corner to discuss the prompt • Students from different corners partner and engage in conversation	L	M	M to H	76
Give Me Five	• A way for teachers to formatively assess students' knowledge of a piece of content • Students hold up the corresponding number of fingers for their level of understanding, ranging from all five fingers ("I got it") to pinky only ("I understand very little)"	L	L	L	96
Give One, Get One	• Students jot down a key idea on an index card • On the signal, they move around the room, verbally and physically giving their idea to a classmate and getting one in return • Continue for a set time period • Entire class engages in conversation	M	L	M	85
Graffiti Wall	• A sheet of paper makes its way around a group • Students write a word or short phrase to capture their thinking about the content • Then the paper is passed in the opposite direction, with each student adding a nonlinguistic representation (illustration) • Continue for as many passes as desired	L	L	M	77

Continued

Name of Strategy	Brief Description	$	T	C	#
Grouping Students	• The teacher uses a variety of fun ways to place students into groups • Example: Distribute geometric shapes and place all the rectangles in one group, triangles in another, etc.	H	M	L	63
Hi, Mac	• Students find a "highly intelligent motivated attentive classmate" to be their partner	L	L	L	63
Hit the Target	• Students record important learnings on half-sheets of colored paper • On the signal students crumple their paper into a ball and try to hit the target: a designated spot on the wall or a container on the floor • After tossing their papers, students retrieve one that is a different color than theirs • Students return to seat, read the responses, and make appropriate comments • Repeat the process • Whole-class conversation follows	L	L	L	77
Human Bingo	• Each student has a handout with different prompts • They find classmates to respond to the prompts by putting their names in the appropriate spaces • Teacher draws names of students at random • Students place a marker on the space if they have that name • Three-in-a-row gets "Human Bingo" • Students whose names are on the winning game board must respond correctly before a winner is declared	L	M	H	44
Hum-dinger	• Students each have a slip of paper with a song title • They hum the song, while they listen to and find others humming the same song • This becomes students' new group	L	M	L	64
I Have, Who Has	• Each student has a card with "I have _____. Who has _____?" written on it • The cards have content-related statements that are sequential • Students respond, "I have _____" when they have the slip that correctly responds to the previous "Who has _____?" • The responses circle back to the first person	L	H	M	64
Inside-Outside Circle	• Students stand in two concentric circles facing each other • A teacher-generated prompt is shared • Each person in one of the circles responds to the corresponding partner in the other circle • Then one (or both) circles rotate a set number of people • The process is repeated so that different pairs respond to the same prompts or different prompts	L	L	M	78

Continued

Name of Strategy	Brief Description	$	T	C	#
Jigsaw	• Content-related material is broken into small, manageable pieces • Each student is given and reads through one piece • Students with the same piece form expert groups and engage in conversation to enhance knowledge and understanding of their piece • One person from each of the expert groups forms a mixed group that discusses the material	M	M to H	H	65
Juggling Our Learning	• Small groups of students stand in a tight circle • One person shares a new learning and tosses a koosh ball to second student • Second student repeats the first learning and adds a new one • Continue until all have had the chance to repeat *all* the previous learnings and then add their own	H	L	L	79
Keeper/ Leaper	• As a way for students to reflect on recent learning, they select one item that is important to them (keeper) and one item that they need to understand more thoroughly (leaper)	L	L	L	96
Key Punch	• Students work as a team and against the clock to touch the keys 1 through 30 sequentially, following three important rules: • All must participate • Only one person in the restricted area at any one time • Keys must be touched in order	L	H	H	66
The Laugh-In Party	• Students mingle around the room • When the music stops, they freeze and pair with a classmate • They make relevant conversation around a teacher-generated prompt for about a minute • The pattern continues for the selected number of prompts	L	M	L	85
Learning Partners	• Each student has a sheet with three to five icons, each one representing a topic related to content and/or fun • The student's task is to find a different partner for each of the icons • When the teacher asks students to get with their "Addition" partner, each student has a partner already chosen	L	M	M	67
Let's Get Ready to … Learn!	• Students respond to two prompts to gauge their background knowledge on a topic of study: • What do you already KNOW about … ? • What do you WANT to learn about … ?	L	L	M	52
Line Up/ Wrap	• Teacher/leader shares a content-related prompt that requires people to take a stand • Students/staff line up shoulder to shoulder, in order from "strongly agree" to "strongly disagree" • The teacher/leader "wraps" the line so the people with the strongest opposing opinions stand opposite each other • Conversation commences	L	L	M	86

Continued

Name of Strategy	Brief Description	$	T	C	#
Links to Learning	• Students record key learnings, new ideas, questions on thin strips of paper • As the strips are completed, they are fastened together to form a paper chain	L	L to M	M	97
Memory Mingle	• Students record a key word on an index card • On the signal, students mix around the room • When time is called, students form trios • Trios use all three words from their cards to write a complete sentence • Trios share their sentences with the rest of the class	M	L	M to H	86
MI Challenge	• Groups of students work together to make a presentation to the class using as many of the multiple intelligences as possible	L	L	H	68
MIP/MVP	• Students choose a key learning as their "Most Important/Valuable Point"	L	L	L	97
The Mixing Bowl	• Students are placed into groups of four and numbered 1 to 4 • Teacher displays a content-related prompt • Groups take a minute to come up with a response. All must understand the group's response • Teacher selects a number from 1 to 4 at random • That student in each group moves clockwise to the next group • The new groups engage in conversation • When new groups have finished, the teacher shares the second prompt • The process is repeated for the number of prompts written	L	L	M to H	87
Musical Bags	• Teacher prepares content-related prompts on slips of paper and places them in a bag • Students sit in small circles and pass the bag around while music is playing • When the music pauses, the person holding the bag removes one of the slips, reads it aloud to the group, and responds • After a minute, the music starts again and the pattern continues for as long as desired	M	H	M	88
Paired Verbal Fluency	• Students stand facing a classmate • Student 1 shares content-related information for 20 seconds while Student 2 listens only • Then Student 2 speaks for 20 seconds giving information *not* shared the first time • Repeat the process for as long as desired, continually decreasing the amount of time to respond	L	L	L	79

Continued

Name of Strategy	Brief Description	$	T	C	#
Puzzling Connections	• Teachers prepare different 8½ × 11 sheets of paper with content-related text and/or illustrations cut into pieces • Students are given a piece (or two) and find partners to complete the puzzle • In this new group, conversation commences around the content conveyed on the completed puzzle	M	H	L to M	70
Racking Up the Points	• Students write everything they can about the unit of study • After a set amount of time, students work in small groups to increase the items on their lists • Next, each student finds a person from a different group and compares lists • They score points for items that are the same and different	L	L	M to H	80
Round the Room and Back Again	• Students write down a key learning, then commit it to memory • Papers and pencils stay at seats • When music starts, students meet each other in pairs and share their learnings • Students continue the pattern, meeting as many different classmates as possible, sharing and listening each time • When time is called, students return to seats and write down as many of the ideas as they can remember	L	L	M	88
Say Something	• Pairs of students are given a teacher-prepared passage with multiple sections • Students read the first section silently • Each person then says something about what they read to each other • Continue for remaining sections	L	M to H	L to M	80
Six-Word Memoirs/ Stories	• Students capture the main ideas from a piece of content using only six words	L	L	H	97
Snowball Review	• Students record important learnings on half-sheets of colored paper • On the signal students crumple their paper into a ball and have a snowball fight • After 20 to 30 seconds, they retrieve a piece of paper that is a different color from their own • Students add comments to the paper and return it to the original owner	L	L	M	39
Spend a Buck	• Students have choice in what to do next • Each students gets a set amount of "bucks" • They spend their money on those topics they choose • The item with the most "bucks" is the focus of the learning	L	M	M	53

Continued

Name of Strategy	Brief Description	$	T	C	#
Stand Up, Sit Down, Write, Write, Write	• Students place an 8½ x 11 blank sheet of paper on their desks • Teacher shares a content-related prompt • On the signal students move around the room, leaving the paper at their seat and discussing the prompt • On the next signal, students choose a seat and write a response to the first prompt • Continue the pattern for the number of prompts with students sitting in a different seat each time • On the last prompt, students return to their original seat to read their classmates' responses, editing if necessary • Handout could be used for review or assessment	L	M/H	M	89
Stepping Out of Line	• Teacher prepares a statement that requires students to take a stand • Students line up, single file, front to back • On the signal students take one step to the left if they agree, one step to the right if they disagree • Students could then be paired for discussion with an opposing partner or one that agrees	L	L	L	89
Team-mates Consult	• Groups of students place writing utensils in a cup • Each student has a list of teacher-generated prompts • Individuals respond to a prompt • Once the group reaches consensus, they use their writing utensils to record their response • The process continues until all prompts have been addressed	L	M	M to H	70
Teenie Tweet	• Using 40 characters or less, students capture the main idea of what they are learning	L	L	L	98
Think-Pair-Share	• Students are presented with a prompt • They think quietly to themselves, then pair with another student and take turns sharing their thinking • *TPSS (Square):* Two pairs of students get together	L	L	L to M	98
Twenty-Second Speech	• Students summarize their work by preparing and delivering a speech that lasts about 20 seconds • Can be done individually or in small groups	L	L	H	98
Two Truths and a Fib	• Three statements are presented to students: two true and one false • Students determine which statement is the fib	L	M	M	53
Uncom-mon Common-alities	• Students work in groups to discover things they have in common • The more unique they are (based on teacher judgment), the more points scored	L	L	M to H	71
Vanity Me	• Students use a template to create their own vanity license plate	M	H	H	54

Continued

Name of Strategy	Brief Description	$	T	C	#
The Wizard	• Students work in small groups as *one* voice to respond to a teacher-generated prompt • The response is given one person at a time to form a coherent answer	L to M	L	M to H	71
Words Alive	• Using individual cards with content-related words, teams of students create one sentence using all of the given words • Then the group presents the sentence to the class in whatever fashion they choose	L	L	M to H	72
Your Sentence Is Up	• Team task is to form a content-related sentence without talking • Teams line up • Students race to the board, one at a time, writing one word related to content, forming a sentence	L	L	M	72

How to Break Out of the Homework Rut!

Homework, homework, homework. Generations of students have lamented that homework will be the end of them. Perhaps those are the voices to which we should listen. Too often the assignments students are given are just not engaging or relevant. When assigned independent work, some students don't understand what they are being asked to do and spend hours trying to finish the assignment. And then there are the phone calls and emails from parents and guardians…

Probably all teachers have assigned the following types of "traditional" homework at one time or another throughout their careers:

- Read pages 120–125. Answer questions 1–5 in your notebook.
- Complete the worksheet.
- Do exercises 1–21 on page 285.
- Research a famous scientist and write a 500-word essay.
- Go to the language lab and listen to three recordings about community life.

Yes, there are times when it is appropriate for teachers to assign work such as the examples above. Let's consider adding a few seriously fun tasks to the repertoire. Thanks to Rick Wormeli for the impetus and for sharing a few unique ideas.

- Choose one innovation created during the Industrial Revolution. What would it look like if it had been invented in the 21st century?
- Open a junk drawer and list twenty-two nouns for things you find there.

- Using the materials you have been studying in science class lately, create some "thing" that uses at least three of them.

- Go grocery shopping with the family. Using the sale flyers, do comparisons of prices.

- Read the chapter on letter writing. Then write a letter that breaks every single rule you learned.

- Sit outside for five minutes and listen. Spend the next five minutes listing all the sounds you hear. Circle your favorite five. Write a poem about one.

- Generate five new classes for the school curriculum. Write a letter to school board members persuading them to implement one.

- Explain how the world would be different if water froze at 15 degrees or 50 degrees Fahrenheit.

- Determine the cost of carpeting the floor of the school auditorium. Include a funky design.

- Write a thirty-second radio spot using George Washington to sell deodorant soap. Work in four facts about his role as a general.

- Make up a game that would help your classmates practice what they have been learning.

- Select one of the letters to the editor in the daily paper and support or dispute the claims made.

- Write a paragraph about your wild Aunt Melba that breaks ten rules of capitalization. The next day students present their paragraphs to see if their classmates can figure out which rules were broken and correct them.

- Pretend to be a 21st century television journalist, reporting live from the battlefield during the Battle of Gettysburg.

- Read Chapter Two of *The Pearl* by John Steinbeck, concentrating on the behavior of Kino. Pick one important decisive action he took and explain what he would have to believe to act the way he did. Then advise Kino. Offer him alternative modes of behavior. What would he have to believe to respond in the alternative manner you chose?

- Add Harry Potter or Katniss Everdeen to the novel you are currently reading. How would the conflict change?
- Create a television commercial that persuades viewers to adopt good personal hygiene habits.
- Design a marketing poster for the school's upcoming musical.

Adapted from Wormeli, R. (2002, February). "One Teacher to Another." *Middle Ground*.

Using Music for Seriously Fun Learning

While it is virtually impossible to get an exact number, it is estimated that 500 million to 1 billion songs have been recorded over the years. While no one has yet to manufacture a device portable enough to hold them all, there are a *lot* of songs that can enhance the learning environment. The music does not necessarily have to be current or recognizable to students. Music from *any* decade will work. It's the beat, rhythm, and tempo that catch the brain's attention.

Music acts as a limbic trigger that changes students' emotions. This trigger impacts students' behavior and can positively affect academic performance. Students tend to remember new learning longer and better when music is involved. Music stimulates learning and helps students recall content.

The following list just scratches the surface of a *very* deep list. Use these suggestions as a start to your lesson design. You will find selections of your own that will work well. Students can also offer suggestions. One caution, though: *screen the songs first*. For additional ideas and suggestions, do a Google search and check the websites of online music stores. What you discover will keep you searching and listening (and probably buying) for hours.

Movement:
- 25 or 6 to 4
- Are You Ready?
- Bugler's Dream (Olympic theme song)
- Car Wash
- Cleanin' Up the Town

- Drive My Car
- Flight of the Bumblebee
- Get on Your Feet
- Good Vibrations
- Hawaii Five-O
- Heat Wave
- Heigh-Ho
- Here Comes the Sun
- Let's Get Loud
- Linus and Lucy (Peanuts theme)
- Locomotion
- Love Shack
- Macarena
- Move Along
- Move It
- Mustang Sally
- Na Na Hey Hey Kiss Him Goodbye
- Peppermint Twist
- Peter Gunn theme
- Pomp and Circumstance
- Star Wars main title
- Surfin' USA
- Takin' Care of Business
- Walkin' on Sunshine

Team-Building:

- All I Wanna Do
- The Best Is Yet to Come
- Celebration
- Getting to Know You
- Get Together
- Happy Days theme

- Happy Together
- Help
- I'll Be There for You (Friends theme)
- We Are Family
- With a Little Help from My Friends
- You've Got a Friend in Me

Reflection/Thinking:
- Brandenberg Concertos (Bach)
- Water Suite (Handel)
- Mozart for Meditation: Quiet Music for Quiet Times
- Music for Thinking (Arcangelos Chamber Ensemble)
- Music for Concentration (Arcangelos Chamber Ensemble)
- Music for Productivity (Richard Lawrence)

Transition:
- 1812 Overture
- 59th Street Bridge Song (Feelin' Groovy)
- Always Something There to Remind Me
- Hang On Sloopy
- Hooked on a Feeling (Blue Swede)
- Movie theme songs (John Williams has written many that will work)
- Rawhide theme
- Rescue Me
- Thanks for the Memories
- TV theme songs (most of these selections are short, so students will have to move quickly to get ready for the next activity before the song ends)
- Unforgettable
- William Tell Overture

Sample Lesson Plans

All the activities, strategies, and ideas presented in *Serious Fun* are designed to give teachers a wide range of choices as they build lessons. What follows are three sample lesson plans. While they target a specific content area at a specific grade level, teachers are encouraged to adapt, adapt, adapt!

Getting the Main Idea

Grade level: 2
Subject: English Language Arts
Standard addressed: CCSS.ELA.RI.2.2: Reading Standards for Informational Text, Key Ideas and Details. Identify the main topic of a multiparagraph text as well as the focus of specific paragraphs within the text
21st-century skills: Critical thinking, collaboration, communication
Learning objective: Students will be able to understand how to determine the main idea and supporting details

Materials needed:

- Brown, Margaret Wise. (1947). *Good Night Moon*. New York: Harper.
- Six bags filled with artifacts, such as the following, and numbered 1 to 6:
  - Bag 1: spoon, bowl, small package of cereal, milk carton, juice box
  - Bag 2: piece of drawing paper, markers, glitter, glue, construction paper
  - Bag 3: sunscreen, sand bucket, shovel, bathing trunks, shells
  - Bag 4: collar, leash, can of dog food, brush, dog toy

- Bag 5: sneakers, ball, glove, baseball cap, T-shirt with a team name
- Bag 6: recipe card, cookie cutter, sprinkles, mixing bowl, spoon, cookie sheet

- Collaborating with the school librarian, secure a large selection of nonfiction books, such as the following:
  - Cowley, Joy. (2005). *Chameleon, Chameleon.* New York: Scholastic.
  - Hudson, Cheryl Willis. (2006). *Construction Zone.* Somerville, MA: Candlewick.
  - Kurtz, K. (2010). *A Day on the Mountain.* Mount Pleasant, SC: Sylvan Dell.
  - One of the American State by State books, such as Raven, Margot. (2002). *M Is for Mayflower.* Ann Arbor, MI: Sleeping Bear Press.

Procedure

Anticipatory set: Show students the book *Good Night Moon* by Margaret Wise Brown and open the lesson with the following question: "How many of you have read the book *Good Night Moon*?" After some of the students raise their hands, ask, "Who can tell me what happens in the book?" Show the students some of the text and illustrations from the book. Conversation continues around one more question: "What is the book about?" Eventually, students should concur that the main idea of *Good Night Moon* is about saying good night.

Say to students, "When you can tell what a book, story, or paragraph is about, you can identify the 'main idea.' A reader does this by looking at the details of a book and seeing how they all fit together. Today we are going to look at main ideas in more detail. You're going to be explorers and dig a little deeper. Get ready to set off on your explorations and see if you can figure out the main idea in some of our reading. So before we start on our search, we want to make sure that you understand what a main idea is."

Show students a bag that has been prepared with a number of objects—for example, conversation hearts, a cutout of Cupid, a love letter from mother to child, red and white hearts, and a Valentine's Day card. Pull the objects one at a time from the bag and have students identify the items out loud. Say that these objects are like the details that point to the main idea. Then ask the students to decide what the main idea of the bag is. Explore their responses, asking how the details (items from the bag) support their suggestions.

Show the group another bag with items—for example, a package of seeds, a trowel, a watering can, gardening gloves, and a bag of carrots. Again, ask the students what the main idea of the bag might be. Ask students to justify their response by explaining how the details support it.

Next, tell the students that they will practice in smaller groups to be sure that everyone can find the main idea. Review the rules for working well in a group; then ask students to line up by birthday (month and day) quickly and quietly. Once in a line, check for accuracy in sequencing. Then divide the line of students into an appropriate number of groups, naming them Group 1, Group 2, Group 3, and so on. Assign a leader in each group. Direct each group to a space where they can meet and give each group one of the bags. The instruction to the group is to find the main idea of the bag. Establish a time limit of five minutes and set a timer. The group members identify the items as the leader pulls them out of the bag one by one. Once all the items are out of the bag, they discuss and identify the main idea of the bag. Circulate and monitor the groups.

After five minutes, check to make sure that each group has determined the main idea. Have the students replace the items in the bags and reconvene as a whole group. Return to the first bag whose main idea was Valentine's Day. Tell the students that the main idea has to be supported by details. If the main idea of the bag is Valentine's Day, what are the details or clues that lead to the main idea?

Repeat the entire process with the gardening bag.

Directions

Tell the class that the task for each group is to display their bag's artifacts and ask the other students to determine the bag's main idea. Determine which group goes first by drawing a numbered popsicle stick from a cup. That group assembles at the front of the class. The members take turns pulling an item (a detail) from the bag and having the other teams identify it. After all the items have been identified, ask the other teams what the main idea is and have them justify their answer. Ask the presenting group if that matches their solution. Repeat the process for the other groups.

Then divide the class into partners and give each a nonfiction book. Ask them to find the main idea of the book and identify the details that support their answer.

Ticket out the door: After this partner activity concludes, ask each student to write down the title of the nonfiction book, the main idea, and two details to support the main idea. Review these tickets if desired.

Assessment: Formatively assess the students' efforts through observation of group work. At appropriate intervals, pause the input of new information and ask students to reflect on their learning by using suitable strategies (e.g., *2-1* or *Teenie Tweet*).

Extension: Asks students to reflect on what elements of a nonfiction book help the reader to determine the main idea.

Negative Five to Five

Grade level: 6
Subject: Mathematics
Standards: CCSS: Math.6NS.7.d: Understanding ordering and absolute value of rational numbers. Distinguish comparisons of absolute value from statements about order.
Standard for Mathematical Practice: Reason abstractly and quantitatively; attend to precision.
21st-century skills: Critical thinking, problem solving, communication
Learning objectives: Students will practice simplifying numerical expressions with positive and negative integers. Students will use logic and mathematical reasoning. Students will write complete equations.
Materials needed: Three number cubes (dice) per team, paper and pencil for each student

Procedure

Anticipatory set: Begin math class by projecting a comic about positive and negative integers and facilitating a discussion about the comic.

Then say, "To support some upcoming work with positive and negative integers, we will need to be very proficient in performing operations with them. To do this, we will be playing a game called

Negative Five to Five." This game is based on a game called *1 to 12*, developed by John Hinton of Math Matters Inc.

Then say, "We'll begin by playing a few rounds together so that you understand the game. The object of the game is to go from –5 to 5 or, if you choose, from 5 to –5 by creating numerical expressions to arrive at *all* eleven of the numbers *in sequence*. To play, you roll three dice and you may choose whether to use any two or all three of the numbers on the dice to reach *each* of the target numbers. You are allowed to make any of the numbers shown on the dice positive or negative. Finally, each of you is to record the complete equation that represents each of the target numbers from –5 to 5 or from 5 to –5. Ready to go? Are you positive? Let's begin!"

Roll three dice. The numbers shown are 5, 1, and 2. Say, "As I look at these three numbers, I see that I could start at either 5 or –5. I'll begin with –5 and work my way up sequentially to 5. What expression could I write that would give me –5?" Think out loud and say, "If I made the 5 that I rolled a –5 and multiplied it by 1 (one of the other numbers that was rolled), the product would be –5. Would that work? I choose not to use the 2 this time. Is there another way to reach –5?" Students respond accordingly. As a model for students, write the complete equation: $-5(1) = -5$.

Next, choose a student to be your opponent. That student rolls the dice and gets 3, 1, and 2. He also chooses to start at –5 and writes the expression $-3 + (-2)(1)$. Ask the class if that works. The student writes his complete equation: $-3 + (-2)(1) = -5$. Ask, "Is there another way to use those three numbers to get –5?" Since the student used all three of the numbers on the dice, he is awarded a bonus point, taking a one-point lead.

It's now your turn to roll the dice again. This time the numbers showing are 5, 2, and 5. Think out loud, "My next target number is –4. I don't see a way to get to that number. Can anyone help me?" The conclusion is that there is no way to reach –4 with these numbers, so the turn passes to the student. At this point, select another student to be the opponent; two or three more rolls are completed as an example. Then display the rules to follow:

- Students will work with a partner. Both partners will have paper and pencil to record their equations.
- Each opponent rolls the three dice. The one with the highest sum goes first.

- The objective is for the students to write numerical expressions that have values from either –5 to 5 or 5 to –5. They must find the numbers sequentially and record a complete equation for each of the eleven target numbers.
- The student rolls three dice and, using the numbers shown, creates an expression. The players may use any two or all three of the dice rolled. A student who uses all three dice to create an expression is awarded a bonus point.
- If a student rolls the dice and cannot create an equation, play passes to the opponent.
- If a student rolls the dice and cannot find an expression but the opponent can, the opponent can take that roll.
- The winner is the first person who moves from –5 to 5 or 5 to –5 in order. In case of a tie, the player with the most bonus points wins.

Review the rules and ask the students, "How can I make the rules clearer for you?" After clearing up any misunderstandings, say, "Get out your Learning Partners sheet and get with your 'Fraction' partner." Once students are paired up and have their dice, pencils, and paper, the game begins. While students play, circulate around the room and help students as needed. Remind students to record their equations as they play.

At the end of the allotted time, facilitate a conversation in order to provide some closure. Project the following six numbered prompts on the screen.

1. What aspects of the game did you find interesting?
2. What strategies did you use to win?
3. What interesting patterns did you notice?
4. If we play again, what might you do differently?
5. Is there a way to change our game to reach the same objective?
6. On a scale of 1 (Not at all) to 5 (Loved it!), how much fun was this game and why?

Have students independently roll a die and respond to the appropriately numbered prompt in their journal. Pair students with a classmate who had a different prompt to discuss their thinking. If desired, ask six different students to share their thinking about each of the six prompts with the whole class.

Assessment: Collect the students' pages of equations and use them to determine which students need additional support, reinforcement, or challenges.

Extension: This game can be set up in a learning center for students to play when they have down time in class. Negative Five to Five can also be played by one student trying to beat an individual time or by multiple players following the original rules.

Las Tres P

Grade level: 10

Subject: Languages other than English (e.g., Spanish)

Standards: Standards for Foreign Language Learning: Preparing for the 21st Century (www.actfl.org/advocacy/discover-languages/advocacy/discover-languages/advocacy/discover-languages/resources-1?pageid=3392)

> **Standard 1.1:** Students engage in conversations, provide and obtain information, express feelings and emotions, and exchange opinions
>
> **Standard 1.2:** Students understand and interpret written and spoken language on a variety of topics
>
> **Standard 1.3:** Students present information, concepts, and ideas to an audience of listeners or readers on a variety of topics

21st-century skills: Accessing and analyzing information, critical thinking and problem solving, collaboration, communication, imagination

Learning objective: Students will be able to communicate to others different aspects of Spanish-speaking cultures through the creation of a video

Materials needed: Computers with Internet connectivity, access to print resources

Procedure

The Three P's

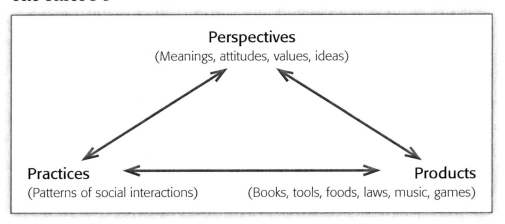

Anticipatory set: Students are completing a unit on Spanish-speaking cultures. Project "The Three P's" graphic on the screen and ask students to think about what they know about the culture of Spanish-speaking nations. What element of a culture would fit into each category of Perspectives, Practices, and Products (http://accelerateu.org/resourceguides/lote.html)? Ask students to count off and remember their number. Review the directions for the strategy.

Inside/outside circle: Have the students with an odd number form an inner circle with their backs to the center and the remaining students with an even number form an outer circle, facing their classmates. Pose the first question, "What is a perspective that would be found in a Spanish-speaking culture?" The inside students respond to their partner first and then the outside students respond. Then have the students on the outside take three steps to their right and greet their new partners.

This time, ask the *outside* students to begin and share a product (book, tool, food, etc.) found in the culture studied; then the inside students respond. Have the inside students move two places to their left and pose a final question to the inside students: "What is a practice that would be found in a Spanish-speaking culture?" First the inside students and then their partners respond.

Students return to their seats. Ask, "Why is it important for us to understand the culture of other nations?" Allow for think time and then ask for responses, facilitating conversation.

Say, "We've talked about how important it is to understand a nation's culture and the elements of that culture. Our task is to help students younger than you come to the same conclusion. Using technology, we are going to create short videos to inform others about aspects of Spanish-speaking culture that fall into each of these categories, Perspectives, Practices, and Products, and why it is important to be open and accepting."

"In order to do this, we are going to form groups of three or four. I have prepared cards that I am distributing to each of you. There are four cards with the word Spain on them, four cards with the word Mexico, four with Chile, four with Panama, four with Costa Rica, and four with Dominican Republic. What do all of these cards have in common?" Have students move about the room to find classmates with matching cards, thus forming teams.

Say, "We have just concluded a unit of study about the culture of Spanish-speaking people. Your task is to inform others about the culture and its importance. Each team will use the tool Go Animate (http://goanimate4schools.com/public_index) to create a five-minute public service announcement (PSA) targeted at middle school students. Each group's card indicates the group's assigned country."

"First, each team needs to research the country on your group's card. The PSA should include at least two pieces of information for each of the categories—perspective, practice, and product—and then explain to your viewers the importance of understanding the culture of different nations. I will distribute the rubric by which your video will be judged. You'll be allotted class time for the next three days to plan and work, although you *will* need to work outside of class. The due date for the assignment is next Friday. The following week, we will have a video premiere. We will post the videos on our class website and discuss how we can get wider distribution."

Distribute and review the rubric, clearing up any questions. Allow time in the remainder of the period for teams to identify what research they will need to find and to plan the storyboard for their video. Have laptops available if teams wish to start their research.

Extension: Students brainstorm ways to get their video to middle school students and what they might do to extend the learning of the middle school students.

Assessment:

	Beginning	Developing	Accomplished	Exemplary
Definition of culture	Does not provide a definition of culture or gives an incorrect definition	Provides a definition of culture that lacks specificity	Provides a correct, complete definition of culture	Gives a correct definition of culture and provides appropriate examples
Brief overview of country	Does not provide either the geographic location or an important fact	Provides geographic location and one or two important facts about the country	Provides geographic location and three important facts about the country	Provides geographic location and four or more important facts about the country
Elements of culture: perspective	Does not include a perspective found in a specific culture	Includes one perspective found in a specific culture	Includes two different perspectives found in a specific culture	Includes three or more different perspectives found in a specific culture
Elements of culture: practice	Does not include a practice found in a specific culture	Includes one practice found in a specific culture	Includes two practices found in a specific culture	Includes three or more practices found in a specific culture
Elements of culture: product	Does not include a product found in a specific culture	Includes one product found in a specific culture	Includes two products found in a specific culture	Includes three or more products found in a specific culture
Appropriate use of *Go Animate* technology	Viewers do not seem to be interested in final product	Video is somewhat engaging to viewers	Video is engaging to viewers while sharing accurate information	Video is highly engaging to viewers while sharing accurate and interesting information
Citation of sources	Does not cite sources	Cites sources but in an inaccurate format	Accurately cites at least three sources to support work	Accurately cites at least four sources to support work